LIVING IN FULL VIEW OF THE GOD OF GRACE

BRUCE YOUNG

LIVING IN FULL VIEW OF THE GOD OF GRACE

ISBN   978-1-953704-17-7   HARDCOVER
ISBN   978-1-953704-18-4   PAPERBACK

Cover Design   Peter Bakelaar, Yusuke "JJ" Matsumura
Design / Editing   Roger W. Lowther

Community Arts Media, LLC
Boston · Tokyo
www.communityarts.jp
info@communityarts.jp

CONTENTS

This book is dedicated to the pastors and wives of the Presbyterian Church of Japan (PCJ), who have sacrificed so much for their churches. They have done so at great personal cost, through tireless hours of ministry in faithfulness to Scripture. My relationship with many of them goes back years to when I was just a young boy living next door to a seminary.

I especially want to thank the many pastors who helped my wife, Susan, and I in our first years as missionaries. I learned so much from living and working with Pastor Horikoshi, Pastor Kurokawa, Pastor Sasaki, Pastor Yanagi, and others.

When we started to work in the Chubu presbytery in the area around Nagano, Japan, we continued to receive help from many pastors in our church planting efforts. I am thankful for their patience with me as I made many mistakes doing ministry in Japan.

I would not have been able to write this book without the encouragement, guidance, and friendship of these men and women, and for them, I am deeply grateful.

PREFACE

I first met Bruce Young as a fledgling missionary learning the basics of life overseas as a Christian worker. In a week-long course called Sonship, he taught that "Christians are the adopted children of God." Simple enough. All Christians know that...but Bruce took me deeper. He repeatedly turned my gaze back to the God of grace to help me understand that God's love is not based on anything that I do. Children do not work for a parent's love—it's a gift that can only be given freely—and neither do the children of God.

The following year, I moved to Japan. In our correspondence and interactions, Bruce and his wife Susan continued to encourage me with grace. They gave me "permission" as a young musician to make mistakes as I experimented with ways to assist church planting through art and culture. "A concert or art exhibit," they assured me, "can be just as effective at communicating the gospel as a worship service or Bible study...and a lot of fun too!" They believed God would certainly use these in Japan. In the years since, even as I did make many mistakes, I saw that they were right. Bruce and Susan taught me how to preach grace to myself as well as to the Japanese people.

During a recent interview, when asked how the arts relate to church planting, Bruce answered, "Well, I think you're really sitting on a mine field!" He laughed as he realized how the image could be taken and quickly clarified, saying, "You're really sitting on gold." I think both images are true. There are inherent "mine field" dangers in communicating the gospel through the arts, but there are also incredible riches.

In "Peace Child," a book about foreign missions among the Sawi people in Papua New Guinea, Don Richardson writes,

> "Ticking away like a time bomb through the ages, that redemptive analogy [of the peace child] was now being detonated by the proclamation of the gospel. From now on, any Sawi who rejected Christ would see himself not as denying an alien concept, but rather as rejecting the fulfiller of the best in his own culture!"[1]

God puts redemptive analogies in every culture, like a "mine field" or "ticking time bomb," detonated by the proclamation of the gospel. Through church planting, we can discover this treasure buried in the soil of Japan and every other soil of the planet. It is available to those who do not yet know him and to those who continually come to know him in deeper and deeper ways.

The symbolism of "trees" in this book as hindrances to the gospel comes from the Bible. Adam and Eve ate from a tree in disobedience and hid behind a tree in fear, blocking their view of the God of grace. But God, seeking to remove those obstacles, called to them, asking, "Where are you?" Then he waited.

Trees in the Bible also symbolize grace. Noah and his family survived the flood by cutting down trees and building an ark. Bitter and undrinkable waters in the wilderness became the sweetest of springs through the casting of a tree. The presence of God followed the Israelites with the Ark of the Covenant built from a tree and gold. All these and more point to the cross, that ultimate tree cut and cast on a hill to bring grace to the world.

Bruce continually orients us to the cross, the tree with power to remove every hindrance to our view of the God of grace. He points out that in the Japanese language itself, the character for the cross (十) occurs within the very center of the character for grace (恵). The "cross" (十) is the core of our identity as Christians, shaping the way we "think" (思) and experience "grace" (恵).

Living in Japan for seventeen years now, I've seen and felt the strong societal pressures to conform and not mess up. For that reason alone, I knew this book was important, but the message was also especially timely for me personally. As of the publication of this book, we are over two years into the COVID-19 pandemic, wreaking havoc on my church, missionary team, and family. My eighteen-year-old son suffers the effects of severe head trauma after a terrible bike accident. My mother is in the last stages of her fight with cancer, and on top of that, though this is insignificant in comparison, I tore a knee ligament and am forced to take a hiatus from playing the pipe organ and giving concerts. Amidst these and other difficulties, Bruce's words greatly encouraged me. Whether you have set foot in the country of Japan or not, I know his words will greatly encourage you as well. Everyone, everywhere, desperately needs grace.

Bruce preaches this grace to our hearts. Even in the most difficult situations, when trees, clouds, rain, or darkness block our view, the mountain still stands. The God of grace still patiently awaits our gaze.

May 2022

Roger W. Lowther
Director, Community Arts Media
Team Leader, Mission to the World

FOREWORD

THIS BOOK WAS ORIGINALLY WRITTEN for the Japanese Christian community, but my fellow missionaries encouraged me to make this book available in English as well, as an example of contextualizing the gospel to a target group. So much more attention needs to be given to this important task!

Contextualization may be the most difficult part of cross-cultural ministry, even more difficult than learning the local language. As I reflect on my years in Japan, I observed early in my ministry the importance of learning the Japanese mindset, what the values were, and why it was difficult to accept Biblical truths. I tried to explain the gospel message in practical and understandable ways, but I became preoccupied with the practical matters of daily life, sermon preparation, and administrative duties, all of which reduced my time with people asking questions and learning about their fears, aspirations, and doubts. I neglected these questions even though I spent many hours in home Bible studies observing Pastor Horikoshi, an extremely effective evangelist in Japan, as he patiently listened and answered questions.

Another reason I neglected my study of Japanese culture was

lack of knowledge on how to do so. I needed practical guides, but it was not until late into my years of ministry that I found some. In one particularly helpful article[1], Tim Keller outlined how to live with the people, meet the people, and spend time with the people. Observe, interact, ask questions, and get feedback, he said. We can learn much by doing so.

Here are some questions I personally found helpful to think about when speaking with people in a specific target group:

1. How do they try to solve problems, and how does the gospel address those problems?
2. What foundational truths do they accept, and which foundational truths help them understand the Bible (i.e., creation, belief in one God, sin, etc.)?
3. What are their top ten objections to Christianity?
4. What are their biggest fears?
5. What statements would unnecessarily turn off listeners (i.e., gender language, cynical remarks of religious leaders, affiliating with specific religious or political parties, nationalism, etc.)?
6. What are the wider concerns of the community?
7. How do they think of the poor and outsiders, and what do their religious beliefs say about them?
8. How do they evaluate artistic excellence?
9. How do people view deeds of justice, mercy, and citizenship?
10. How do people respect, trust, and listen to those in authority?
11. What are the stories and folklores told by this culture that reflect moral values and dreams of deliverance?

There are so many more I could list.

Through the English version of this book, I hope to encourage more dialogue within the missionary community about these topics. How can we engage adopted cultures through gospel application and ask, "What blocks their view of the God of grace in *this* culture?"

INTRODUCTION

ONE OF THE MOST BEAUTIFUL MOUNTAINS in the world is Japan's magnificent Mt. Fuji. Standing 12,389 ft above sea level, few mountains appear so perfectly shaped and to such extraordinary heights.

For those of us growing up in Japan, Mt. Fuji is far more than a tourist attraction. We see Fuji-san (富士山) not only as a mountain but as Fuji-san (富士さん) the person as well.

I recall waking on cold winter mornings as a child and immediately going to the window to see the mountain glow in the early morning sun. After strong typhoon winds blew away summer moisture and smog, it always stood there in clear sight, even at 60 miles away.

As an adult too, Mt. Fuji holds a special place for me. Whether sailing into Yokohama harbor, speeding by on the *shinkansen* bullet train, driving the Tomei expressway, or flying overhead in a plane, the sight of this mountain never fails to bring me joy.

One fall morning many years ago, Mt. Fuji appeared before me while driving to Lake Yamanaka. It stood capped with a blanket of snow against a deep blue sky. As I got closer, the shape and color became even more distinguishable. But suddenly, something took this enjoyment away. The road ran against a long line of fir trees that completely blocked my view of the mountain. I tried to look around, over, and through the trees, but I could not see it even though I knew the mountain was still there. Then a question flashed through my mind that I still remember to this day. "If the beautiful 'mountain' I am trying to enjoy is the God of grace, what are the 'trees' in my life that block my view of this amazing God?"

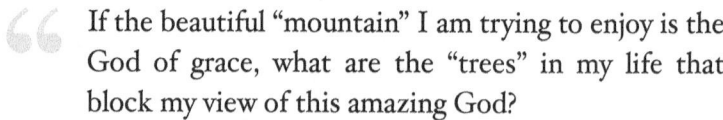

> If the beautiful "mountain" I am trying to enjoy is the God of grace, what are the "trees" in my life that block my view of this amazing God?

This book is an attempt to answer that question for Japanese believers. Christians in Japan have their own particular set of challenges, and we need to be aware of what these "trees" are to prevent them from robbing our joy of knowing God. The mountain we must not lose sight of in daily life does not change from nation to nation or culture to culture, but those things that make it hard to keep our eyes on Him do.

When we come to a greater understanding of what blocks our view of our heavenly Father, we become greater worshipers of Him. When we live in full view of the God of grace, He changes our hearts so that these trees grow smaller, less distracting, and fewer in number.

This book attempts to help keep our eyes focused on God by answering four simple questions from the perspective of living in Japan.

1. Who is God?
2. What blocks our view of God?
3. How are we changed when we look at God?
4. How can we be continually motivated to look at this God of grace?

May my attempt to answer these questions help all of us live with more confidence and joy as we grow in our personal relationship with this God of grace.

CHAPTER 1

WHO IS GOD?

THE ONE TRUE GOD IS THE CREATOR GOD

J apan does not have a history of believing in a Creator God, so Japanese people often have difficulty understanding who He is. The reason for this becomes evident when we look at what society has believed and taught for centuries. There are many traditions and superstitions about who God is, and these traditions create much doubt and confusion. Growing up in Japan, I remember hearing a phrase about God repeated many times:

Even the head of a sardine can be god
イワシの頭も信心から

Little is said about creation in Shinto teaching. All living things have a spirit and are a god. People too become gods when they die. Under Buddhist teaching, we hear from Oshaka-sama (Buddha) about respect and honor but little is said about creation. Today, students are taught that the world came into existence through the process of time plus chance. While this is called *shinkaron* (creation theory), it is not presented to the students as a *ron* (theory) but as scientific fact. Though claimed to be science, there are many assumptions that simply cannot be supported. In Shintoism, the sun goddess shaped the islands of Japan. In Buddhism, followers welcome back spirits of the dead in the August festival called *Obon*. A mixture of ideas make Japanese superstitious and lead them to say, "I believe there's some higher power" without being able to explain what that means.

For those of us who have rejected these commonly held views and believe in the God of the Bible as the Creator of all things, we are sad to see His honor given to theories and ideas that deny His existence. To deny God as the Creator Lord is like going to an art gallery and looking at one beautiful picture after another with the artist's name scratched out and over it written, "Product of Time Plus Chance." Moving from the art museum and out to the street, we would be confused to see a Toyota car emblem replaced by a seal indicating the car was made by "Time Plus Chance." What an insult to the artist, engineer, and builder to have their name removed and give credit to something else as the producer. It is illegal to mislabel products, and the law will bring consequences. Examples of art and a car emblem are man-made and are simple to make compared to the creation of an atom, the human body, or the vast universe. Yet, Darwinian evolution contends that these too are to be marked "time plus chance."

In natural selection, we are told to make giant leaps of faith to believe the world was shaped without a designer or builder. In Shintoism and Buddhism, we are asked to believe fairy tales that have nothing to do with science and are inconsistent with what we see in the world around us. Darwinian evolution claims that the beauty of the earth is the product of chance, while Shintoism and Buddhism ask us to worship anything beautiful, such as majestic Mt. Fuji, without giving credit or honor to the One who created it.

WAYS WE CAN SEE GOD

When we see the world in all its beauty, we know that the Creator God is beautiful. The Old Testament states that we know Him through His creation.

"The heavens declare the glory of God, and the sky above proclaims his handiwork." (Psalm 19:1)

The New Testament states that we can see God so clearly through His creation that we are not excused in denying Him.

"For his invisible attributes, namely, his eternal power and divine nature, have been clearly perceived, ever since the creation of the world, in the things that have been made. So they are without excuse." (Romans 1:20)

We see the beauty of God not just through nature but through history as well. We are not asked to believe in fairy tales that did not really happen but through clearly documented events. The story of the nation of Israel is an example of God's kindness and mercy. He took a small, rebellious people, named them Israel, and saved them from Egypt, the most powerful nation on earth. Then He cared for them and forgave them in spite of their repeated rebellion of forgetting His commands and turning to other false gods. And finally, over 1,400 years later, God became flesh, a man in human form. He became one of us in order to save us from punishment for our rebellion and sin. He bore the sins of the world and was killed on the cross for our punishment. This is the most beautiful picture of love, mercy, and sacrifice ever seen! We see God's beautiful love not just in His creation but because of His loving sacrifice for us demonstrated throughout history.

God is beautiful, but this is not all that makes God unique. God is also personal and not distant like the gods of the religions and belief systems of Japan. When Shintoism talks about spirits, it creates a sense of fear. These spirits can be angered by our actions and bring misfortune. Gods are defined as elements of nature like a majestic tree or mountain to produce peaceful thoughts and a sense of oneness with nature, but they have no personal relationship with us. Buddhism has a founder who never referred to himself as available to be with all who followed him. Rather, he taught the dangerous nature of the physical world and encouraged people to remove themselves from it. The teacher left behind a set of eight steps to the path of escape from the world. By keeping these steps, people can attain the ideal state of mind, which is said to bring the deepest meaning in life.

GOD IS A PERSONAL GOD

Only in Christianity do we find a God who desires to have a personal relationship with us. For obvious reasons, Darwinian evolution does not promote a sense of intimacy to some power. It is a belief based on cold assumptions intended to eliminate any need for a Creator God, let alone a personal one. The traditional religions of Japan promote a set of rules in order to live a good life, but these teachings result in superstitions that are scary and unrelated to love and trust. On the other hand, the God of the Bible is personal because He became one of us to save us and will someday return in physical form as the Lord of the universe. He is a God who does not bring fear but hope and joy. He will fix this broken world and will give us hearts to love Him perfectly. He is Immanuel, God with us. He wants us to know Him as the Good Shepherd. He is our Father and we are His children, His loved ones. He promises to always be with us and has left with us His Holy Spirit who dwells within every believer. We are not orphans but God's children. God is not only with us but dwells within us.

We are made in the image of God but are not a miniature version of Him, small gods like Shintoism teaches. Rather, we are created with a mind, soul, and capacity to believe in Him, to live for Him, and to have a relationship with Him. Our lives have meaning and worth, and we are able to enjoy God and His creation because we share in His image. God made us to worship and obey Him and are uniquely different from all of creation. God put us over creation with the God-given responsibility to manage nature while we enjoy living in it. He commands us to care for nature, and we fulfill our calling when we are good stewards of the earth. In spite of our rebellion, by God's grace our capacity to be creative was not taken away, so we are able to enjoy the beauty in art, music, storytelling, and a host of other activities such as dancing, sports, and hiking! It is truly amazing that God seeks us out for intimate contact and relationship with Him and that He delights in our enjoying Him and His nature.

God is also unique in the way He chooses to reveal Himself to us. The universe certainly displays the glory of God, but it does not enable us to know Him personally. For that, we have been given the most clear and understandable view of God through His Son, Jesus Christ, and through the Bible. Though Jesus lived over 2,000 years ago, we can know Him intimately because we have a perfectly preserved historical record of Jesus's life and teaching. In the Bible, we learn how He embodies the perfect nature of God's love and His character. Christ is the perfect reflection of the Father in His thoughts, actions, and love for all people. This is why God inspired men throughout the ages to write down what He intended for us to learn from Him. The Bible has one unique, consistent message even though written over a period of 1,500 years by 40 different authors. This account has been written down accurately and without mistake, and we should be thankful for this wonderful, irreplaceable, and necessary gift of His Word. We know God personally as a friend because the Word became flesh and dwelt among us through Jesus Christ. This gives us the confidence to say that He knows us and can meet all of our needs.

CHAPTER 2

WHAT BLOCKS OUR VIEW
OF GOD?

THE GOD OF GRACE MEETS ALL OUR
EMOTIONAL NEEDS

The trees that block our view of God often come from within. They are emotional needs we feel, and until they are met God seems distant and not real to us. This is not only true of non-Christians but Christians as well in spite of the way the Lord has demonstrated His power and love through creation, history, the Bible, and His Son Jesus Christ. We are amazed and thankful but unless we experience what God has done for us, we will be plagued with doubts that He is there or even that He cares. In these moments of doubt, we need to see that, as our Maker, He understands we have emotional needs and He knows exactly how to meet them. It is no wonder that as the One who made us, He knows how to do this. God has chosen to meet our needs on a personal basis to fill the emptiness in our hearts and to prevent us from feeling alone, lost, and hopeless.

On that morning as I was driving to Mt. Fuji, I experienced a sense of emptiness when the row of fir trees blocked my view of the mountain. But in a more significant way, when we lose sight of what the God of grace has done for us personally, we become discouraged and weak in our faith. God seems distant, unreachable, uncaring, and cruel until our eyes are opened and our hearts are touched by the awareness of His gracious act of love.

What are the conditions of our heart that make God seem so distant? And how does He deal with our emotional needs through the gospel message lessening their power over us? In this chapter, we identify eight felt needs that we have, how this condition affects us, and how God graciously provides for us. But in order to take a look at our needs, first we must take a realistic and honest look at ourselves.

A REALISTIC VIEW OF SELF

When we become Christians, we do not cease to struggle. We find it hard at times to believe we are really forgiven and loved by God, especially when we continue to fail to put Him first and love others. Rather than be reassured, we experience all sorts of negative feelings that make us lose sight of God. This is why we are often tempted to say, as so many do in Japan, "I'm embarrassed to call myself a Christian because I'm not a good person." We often walk around as though there is a dark and heavy cloud over our heads. When we are with other believers, we might feel safe to talk openly about struggles but usually we just struggle on our own. We have a built-in fear we might be discovered. And this fear is instilled in all of us from living in a society that from childhood teaches everyone to be very conscious of those around us and not behave in a way that brings shame. We hear our mother's voice motivating us to behave with, "People are watching so don't embarrass yourself!" This training from early childhood affects how we view and interact with others and even God. It explains why as believers we still struggle with being honest and open.

But as children of God, we have been given the means to handle negative feelings of alienation, condemnation, guilt, loneliness, death, hopelessness, inadequacy, and separation. Each one acts as a "tree" that casts long shadows over us and blocks our view of the God of grace. Only through the power of the Holy Spirit through the gospel of Christ, can the trees be removed.[1]

TREE #1 – ALIENATION

The words *nakama* (insider) and *nakama hazure* (outsider) are important words in Japan. Nobody wants to be excluded and left on their own. We all need to be accepted by at least one small group and will expend a lot of effort to stay in that group. This can be observed most clearly in the behavior of children who have not yet learned to be discrete about it. They are quick to determine who is inside and who is outside.

We read every day about the effects this has on children. When I was a child, I hated having kids point their finger at me and say, "*Gaijin da!*" ("Foreigner!"). I wanted to be one of them and not be pointed out as different. This emotional desire to blend, not stand out, and be accepted as one of the members of the group explains why our daughter was embarrassed when her different looking parents showed up at her school. She wanted to blend in and be accepted, but she feared having her *gaijin* parents remind her schoolmates that she was a foreigner.

Children can be cruel in the way they determine who is in their group. If a child is overweight, a poor student, stutters, or is shorter or taller than others, they will often be picked on for being different. And there's nothing the suffering child can do about it. This bullying has led to the recent increase in numbers of children who stay home and refuse to attend school. They are one of the many *futoukou* children, a term which has no English equivalent. Feelings of alienation profoundly affected their lives to the point they can no longer attend school.

This kind of shame and rejection is not unique to children, but adults are more sophisticated about it. We have all faced rejection from unreturned phone calls, becoming the subject of gossip, and no longer being invited. Feelings of loneliness from having been unjustly rejected turns to resentment and self-doubt. We ask, "What did I do wrong to have them reject me?"

Emotions from alienation run deep in one's heart but they do not always come from the isolation or rejection of others. They can come from deep within even when we are in the middle of a large crowd or sitting alone in a quiet place. At such times, we realize that these feelings of alienation are not confined to how people treat us but come from deep down and are something that we are born with. It is as though these feelings are telling us in a quiet way that something is not right. Something is missing in life even when we have good friends and lack nothing. It's hard to identify why we feel this way. Many deny there is any such hole in their lives and instead look to friends or successes to lessen the emptiness.

The Bible helps us understand why we feel this alienation. We are created in the Creator's image, and He made us to have a relationship with Him. He is the only One who can fill the vacuum in our hearts. But there is a barrier between God and us because we know that our lives do not measure up to God's standards. While many deny it, subconsciously we feel that His standards are high, and thus we are unqualified to know Him. Alienation from God is connected to the shame that we feel. Shame makes us feel unqualified to know God, and the less we know God the more we feel alienated.

The world has two approaches to this problem. One person denies that there is a God and thus thinks there is no reason for shame. The other believes in a god but not one that is approachable or a part of his or her life. In either case, God is at a distance. They cannot see the God of grace.

The answer to man's alienation and shame lies in the God who moves toward us. Scripture says that before the foundation of the world God chose us and determined a way to do away with our alienation and shame. His plan was to allow His own Son, Jesus Christ, to experience shame and alienation from His Father so that as His chosen ones and His special children, we will no longer have to live under the struggle of shame and alienation.

Alienation and shame lose their powerful effect over us when we see that we are no longer "outsiders" but brought into the family of our Heavenly Father, who chose us in spite of what we have done. Jesus took upon Himself the shame of rejection when God turned His face from His Son on the cross. And now He will never turn His face away from us!

We can observe how Jesus dealt with the alienation and shame Peter felt after his failure by denying Jesus three times. The first thing Jesus asked Peter after his death and resurrection was not guilt inducing but affirming. He asked Peter three times, "Do you love me?" Peter answered Jesus each time with the answer, "Yes." It would have been perfectly right for Jesus to alienate Peter and make him full of shame for his betrayal, but instead He reassures Peter that he is forgiven and fully restored. Jesus restores him into the circle of disciples by saying, "Feed my sheep." Peter continues as a disciple to work for God's kingdom as a full member of the chosen group of twelve disciples, even to become their leader!

Paul identifies all followers of Christ as "aliens." As Christians living in Japan where we are such a minority, we feel like aliens every day. When others find out we are Christians, we are often treated differently. The only way we can live under this pressure is to remember the amazing story that Jesus has placed us into His family and treats all of us in Christ the same way! Like Peter, we fail Jesus and we deserve to be disowned by Him. Instead we are secure because He has dealt with the shame and alienation through His Son. We are secure because we freely receive His gift of mercy and grace. His acceptance and welcome are not earned by our good works.

Our feeling of alienation and shame can become a "tree" that blocks our view of God. But when we turn to the God of grace and see His infinite love and see how He has made it possible for us to be His special children, then we will be renewed with courage to know He is the mountain that is always there!

Key Verse

"And [Christ] came and preached peace to you who were far off and peace to those who were near. For through him we both have access in one Spirit to the Father. So then you are no longer strangers and aliens, but you are fellow citizens with the saints and members of the household of God." (Ephesians 2:17-19)

TREE #2 – CONDEMNATION

People carry in their hearts a fear of condemnation. To verify the truth of this statement all we need to do is attend a funeral or listen to people talk about the deceased person. We never hear negative things spoken even if it is obvious to all the people present that the deceased was selfish and mean. Only respectful and polite words are used such as, "He was a hard worker. Though he wasn't perfect, he did his best. Now he's at peace in heaven."

One reason people act this way at a funeral is because of their fear of condemnation. They fear others will speak badly about them at their funeral. They want people to say, "He or she is at peace in heaven now." Even agnostics who do not believe in God or heaven feel the same way. While they may think, "I'm not afraid," when it comes to a funeral everyone knows their words betray them.

We do not like to talk about condemnation at any time, not just at funerals. And so, one of the hardest things for people to understand about the God of the Bible is that He hates sin and will condemn the unrepentant sinner. The Bible teaches that those who reject Jesus Christ will be condemned by God.

"For God did not send his Son into the world to condemn

the world, but in order that the world might be saved
through him. Whoever believes in him is not condemned,
but whoever does not believe is condemned already,
because he has not believed in the name of the only Son of
God." (John 3:17–18)

All who do not accept God's pardon through faith are subject
to His anger. The unbelieving person prefers to believe in a god of
love, mercy, and patience, and not in a god who gives eternal
punishment. They prefer to create a god in their minds according
to what they would like. And yet, while they say it is unfair for
God to judge people for their actions, they live in constant judgment and condemnation of those around them. They have a long
list of people such as fellow workers, company boss, neighbors,
corrupt politicians, thoughtless relatives, or even a spouse. They
sit in judgment over these people and would be glad to see them
punished in some way. And yet, while they condemn others, they
think it is wrong for there to be a God who would punish people
for their evil thoughts and actions.

Christians can also suffer from the fear of God's condemnation. This fear can be a "tree" that blocks our view from seeing the
God of grace. We may not fear the condemnation of those around
us like we used to because we know God's forgiveness in Christ,
but when we see how we fail to love and obey Him, we can fear
God. This fear is often evident on the faces of Christians. They
look as though there is a dark cloud over them that comes from a
sense of inadequacy. It conveys the message, "I should be better
and I don't deserve to be happy."

Have you felt this way? We can be like the person in the
temple with Jesus who says repeatedly, "God be merciful to me a
sinner," but cannot believe he or she is forgiven and instead feels
rejected. While it is true we should be aware of our sins, we
must also joyfully receive God's forgiveness. If we don't, we
remain under the cloud of God's condemnation. He does not

want us to live under this cloud because it will block our view of His grace!

As a Christian, how can we deal with this underlying sense of condemnation? Society's answer to this question is inadequate. From childhood and years of schooling and the pressures of society, people are taught they can avoid this fear by being a good respectable person who conforms to social norms. Japan is a country with highly developed norms to follow. What is acceptable and polite is clearly defined. These norms may change from generation to generation, but they must be kept. The pressure to conform and be polite has made Japan a well-organized and safe society. But why do they still feel inadequate? Because while they can change behavior, they cannot change the heart, and it is the heart that sows seeds of fear.

One day, I observed how conformity to social norms can produce a cold and judgmental heart. I was sitting in a commuter train. Across from me, an elderly woman sat beside a young teenage girl who was putting on make-up. My eyes were on the woman watching from the corner of her eye as the girl took out a kit, looked into a mirror, and started putting on eye shadow and lipstick. It was easy to see how the young lady's actions upset the older woman. Her eyes were frowning. Her face was stern. I could tell she was biting her tongue to keep from scolding her and saying, "You're so rude! No polite, respectable young girl would do this! I certainly would not have put on makeup in public when I was your age!"

What caused this older woman to have such a cold, judgmental attitude towards the young girl? It was because she thought the girl was being socially rude. It is hard for people to be gracious and forgiving with rules of politeness, when they think they themselves are keeping the rules. Rules of politeness may build an ordered society but cannot change the heart.

God's way of dealing with the fear of condemnation is completely different from the way humans deal with it. We attempt to rely on good deeds to avoid rejection and criticism, but this avoidance grows a harsh and critical heart. God's way of dealing with this is to transform our hearts by freely giving a great gift. He declares we are forgiven even though we are guilty and sinful. His holy nature demands that He hate sin and must condemn the unrepentant sinner. All people would agree that Aum Shinrikyo's leader, Shoko Asahara, was judged rightly for killing people with sarin gas in the Tokyo subway in 1995. The nation would have responded in anger if the judge determined that since he liked Asahara, he released him without punishment in spite of what he had done!

As the supreme judge, God has a right to demand justice on those who commit wrongdoing. While not one of us would say we are perfect, most would say, "I'm not as bad as Shoko Asahara and therefore don't deserve such punishment from God. I'm a better person than Asahara and try to do my best, so God will accept me rather than punish me." Jesus, however, does not agree with this way of thinking. He says that God's standard is too high for any to pass the test of judgment. He says that when we break one of His rules it is as though we have broken all of them.

> "For truly, I say to you, until heaven and earth pass away,
> not an iota, not a dot, will pass from the Law until all is
> accomplished. Therefore whoever relaxes one of the least
> of these commandments and teaches others to do the same
> will be called least in the kingdom of heaven, but whoever
> does them and teaches them will be called great in the
> kingdom of heaven." (Matthew 5:18–19)

According to God's standard we are all condemned because we have broken many of His commandments. But God is rich in grace and mercy and has made it possible for us to be removed from His condemnation. He did this by placing our sins on Jesus on the cross, so that we need not be punished. Because Christ was condemned, we no longer have to fear condemnation.

When we truly come to the place where we understand that God's condemnation is removed because of what Christ has done for us, three things happen in our hearts. One, the fear of God's rejection is removed. That dark cloud of inadequacy and guilt is lifted not because we have become a better person, but because God has removed our guilt through His Son Jesus Christ. We have a new status as forgiven. Two, the fear of rejection by others is lessened because we understand that the only One who really matters, our Savior Jesus Christ, no longer condemns us and accepts us as His own! This helps us to bear the pain of human rejection. Three, our attitude toward others has changed from being proud and self-centered to humble. We deserve judgment but instead have received forgiveness as a gift. We have no reason to be proud or judgmental of others.

When we understand that the fear of God's condemnation is removed from us, we are able to be honest and admit our sin. The story of Simon the Pharisee and the woman of the street in Luke 7 is a good lesson of how God works in hearts to bring humility and repentance. Simon was proud of his record of keeping all the rules. He had no fear of being judged by God. In fact, from observing his critical attitude, we can see that he thought that he was even more righteous than Jesus! He was highly judgmental because Jesus let a woman of the street touch him. On the outside, Simon looked like a holy person, but on the inside his heart was cold and condemning of both Jesus and the woman.

Simon is an example of what pride does to a heart. In this story, it is the woman who is praised by Jesus because she admitted she was a sinner and unworthy. In her heart, she knew that Jesus loved sinners and the needy. She also knew that Jesus would accept her and love her as no one else had ever done. This is why she came to Jesus in thankfulness and worship by kissing His feet and hair with her tears and pouring expensive ointment on Him. Jesus turned to Simon the Pharisee and asked him a question that addressed the problem of his cold heart. Jesus asked, "If two people had debts to repay which person would be more appreciative and thankful, the one whose large debt is forgiven or the one with a small debt?" Simon answered correctly by saying the one with the larger debt, but he did not see himself as having the larger debt. He thought that his debt was small because he kept the rules faithfully. This explains why he was cold and unloving. In contrast to Simon, the woman knew she had many sins. Accordingly, Jesus answered the crowd, "Therefore I tell you, her sins, which are many, are forgiven—for she loved much. But he who is forgiven little, loves little" (Luke 7:47).

This then is the formula for overcoming our fear of condemnation. When we admit to and confess our sins to God and receive His great gift of forgiveness, we are humbled, and God enables us to love Him and others more deeply. But when we refuse to admit our sins, we think too highly of ourselves. Rather than receive God's love and grow in our love for Him and others, we remain proud and judgmental like Simon the Pharisee.

The fear of condemnation is lessened when we see Jesus having been condemned for us. Therefore, we can stand before Him forgiven. Our fear of condemnation is not only lessened, but our hearts are changed to be more thankful and loving as we see how much God loves us by forgiving us of our great debt to Him.

Christians can face God's condemnation without fear because they look to what Jesus has done. God's judgment is a positive message, a sweet aroma for those who rest in Christ.

"Thanks be to God, who in Christ always leads us in triumphal procession, and through us spreads the fragrance of the knowledge of him everywhere. For we are the aroma of Christ to God among those who are being saved and among those who are perishing, to one a fragrance from death to death, to the other a fragrance from life to life. Who is sufficient for these things?" (II Corinthians 2:14-16)

Christ cut down the "tree" of condemnation and enables us to see the God of grace more clearly.

Key Verse

"But God, being rich in mercy, because of the great love with which he loved us, even when we were dead in our trespasses, made us alive together with Christ—by grace you have been saved—and raised us up with him and seated us with him in the heavenly places in Christ Jesus, so that in the coming ages he might show the immeasurable riches of his grace in kindness toward us in Christ Jesus. For by grace you have been saved through faith. And this is not your own doing; it is the gift of God, not a result of works, so that no one may boast. For we are his workmanship, created in Christ Jesus for good works, which God prepared beforehand, that we should walk in them." (Ephesians 2:4-10)

TREE #3 - GUILT

The word "guilt" in Japan is usually reserved for someone who has committed a serious crime. For this reason, we hear more talk about fear than guilt. Most people think it applies only to people like Shoko Asahara the leader of the Aum Shinrikyo who was responsible for the deaths of people exposed to sarin gas in the subway. He was found guilty and given the death sentence for this terrible act. In the minds of many, the word guilt is restricted to this sort of evil action. Therefore, they do not think of themselves as guilty for much less serious actions. A person is pronounced guilty only when he or she breaks a criminal law and is prosecuted.

There is another category of action that might have less damaging consequences but is harmful nevertheless. Our society and we as individuals make up rules that we are to keep in order to be considered respectable. When these social norms are broken, the offender is not referred to as guilty but impolite, rude, insensitive, selfish, and bad. Many other such words are used. This interpretation comes from a purely horizontal, person-to-person perspective based on how to behave in society. When there is no history of a belief in a Creator God who created the world and established rules, only man-made rules are relevant. In the absence of a Creator God who makes rules to live under, Japan has established its own set of rules that determine who is an honest, respectable, polite, and hard-working person. Over the years, these rules have become sophisticated and numerous. And when they are broken, rather than using the term "guilty," words like shameful, dishonest, disrespectful, and lazy are used. Society treats such people harshly. They are often criticized and ostracized. Because there has not been the vertical consideration of a God who determines rules, society determines what is right and wrong from a strictly horizontal level.

One result of rules determined on a social, horizontal level is that they undergo modification and change over time. Take for example the social norm about women not smoking in public because it is rude. Today this has changed to be acceptable for any adult to smoke if it is in an appropriately designated area.

On a more significant level, there have been changes in rules that have directly affected who will live and who will not. Take for example the national law on abortion. Before the end of WWII, it was illegal to abort a child. The country was anxious for families to have many children to support the war effort. But immediately following the war, there was a serious problem with the surge in population. The country was poor from the effects of the war. To deal with the fast growth in the population, the abortion law was changed to allow it if the mother could demonstrate that giving birth would place undue stress in her life. Now over 60 years later, this law has not changed. Consequently, over the first three decades, the average annual abortion rate was over one million per year. Today even with numerous birth control methods available, the number is still over 300,000 a year. One out of every three pregnancies end in premature termination!

Which law can have a stronger effect on the human soul, the one society determines (such as the abortion law) or the one written on the human heart by the God who created it? From looking at the example of the abortion law, we can see that God's law is more powerful. Society has determined that it is acceptable to kill unborn babies, but women who have done so struggle in their hearts with the pain of having done something wrong. This is evident from observing the tens of thousands of *mizuko jizos*. These are small stone images of children dressed in red found all around Japan. Temples invite prayer for the spirits of aborted babies for money. Grief, fear, confusion, and hope for forgiveness are often the motivation to pay a priest to comfort their aborted child and soothe their own conscience. An awareness remains in the human heart that even though such action is legal, it is wrong and brings a deep sense of guilt.

If a citizen can keep the law and still feel guilty, where then does this guilt come from? It comes from deep within because God gave us a soul made to live in accordance with what He determined is right. It helps to see there is a higher moral law and that it is incorrect to deny what the Bible says. When we break God's laws, we are guilty and subject to punishment. And these laws are not the same as society's laws. Until we understand this, we hold a false notion that we don't need to be forgiven by God. But when we look at God's standards, we understand how very different and more demanding they are.

Jesus said, "Do not kill" and "Do not steal." We would be quick to say we have never committed these crimes. But according to Jesus, hating or lusting is the same as killing and stealing. Since we have all done this in our hearts, we have not obeyed God. The standards are so high they cannot be kept!

The summary of God's law is to "love God and love your neighbor as yourself." But this is impossible. We break the commands of God and are therefore "guilty." We know this to be true, but rather than admitting it and asking for help we suppress the truth.

> "For the wrath of God is revealed from heaven against all ungodliness and unrighteousness of men, who by their unrighteousness suppress the truth." (Romans 1:18)

The Spirit must work in our hearts so we can be humble enough to admit the truth about ourselves. Without this, our natural tendency is to look to our good works and say, "Since I haven't killed someone or stolen anything, I am OK!" When we depend on our own goodness to pass God's test, we are guilty of sinning against God because He created us to trust in Him rather than depending on our own actions.

Trying to live independent of God's love and grace is a great sin. Our efforts to cover guilt become a "tree" that blocks our vision of the glory of the God of grace. The guilt that comes from either refusing to admit sin or refusing to go to God in repentance, makes him seem distant.

If guilt is a result of our own actions, and we cannot get rid of it on our own, where can we turn? The story of man's first sin answers this question. Adam and Eve were created without sin but chose to serve themselves rather than God. This is when they first experienced guilt. When God approached, they were afraid, covered themselves, and tried to hide. But God did not allow them to live hopelessly with this guilt. Instead, He promised to provide a solution. It required that Adam and all of us turn to God to fix us rather than depend on ourselves.

To show how our guilt was to be removed, God instructed them to take the life of a sheep and sacrifice it on behalf of themselves. The animal was the substitution provided to show that sin required punishment of death and that someone else would pay for our sins. This did not mean that an animal's life was equal to the life of a human, but it pointed to what God would do through His Son in the future. Through the shed blood of a sheep offered up in faith to God, that person was considered righteous. When I first learned the Chinese character for "righteousness" (義) adopted in the Japanese language, I was moved to see how it is made by placing the character for "sheep" (羊) directly on top of the character for "myself" (我). It makes me wonder if this concept of redemption was directly learned from Jewish merchants along the Silk Road and then captured in the language.

This Old Testament background helps us understand why John the Baptist called out when he saw Jesus for the first time, "Behold, the Lamb of God, who takes away the sin of the world!" The Spirit led him to make this declaration that Jesus became man to die for the sin of mankind to fulfill the symbolism of the sacrificial lamb in the Old Testament. Jesus's death and not the death of sheep would pay for the punishment required for our guilt so that we could be declared righteous. As an innocent and sinless human being, Jesus grew up never disobeying His Father in heaven and was therefore the perfect sacrifice for mankind. He died on the cross and was buried, but on the third day was raised to life, living proof that the penalty for Adam's and our sins are fully paid for. God is satisfied with the perfect sacrifice of His Son. God the Father looks on us as forgiven in Christ, righteous and clean. Our hearts are as white as snow.

Because this forgiveness is something that Christ has done, we can believe two things. One, we will never have to pay for these punishments again. Two, He not only paid for our sin's punishment but has also given something we can never do for ourselves. He gave us His own righteousness. He has not only washed us clean from the guilt of sin, but God takes all the obedient, pure, holy, and perfect acts of Christ and writes them over each one of His children.

Visualize a white board in front of the room. When it is said that God washes us as clean as snow, the teacher takes the white board and wipes away all our sinful acts until it is completely white. But this is not an entirely accurate condition of how we look to God. For He not only wipes the board clean, He takes all of Christ's righteous acts throughout His perfect life and writes them over us! The God of grace adds to us all the righteousness of His Son, Jesus Christ.

"For our sake [God] made [Christ] to be sin who knew no sin, so that in him we might become the righteousness of God." (II Corinthians 5:21)

Now all those perfect acts of Jesus in obeying His Father and in loving people around Him, even those who hated and killed Him, are written over our whiteboard of life.

This is the reason why we as Christians have a hard time getting out from under the cloud of guilt. We understand that God is love and forgives us when we repent, but we still remember our sins and feel obligated to fix them. We may have even tried to fix them but since we cannot, we feel inadequate, shamed, and guilty. The only way to deal with guilt is to claim we are covered with Jesus's perfect acts of righteousness. We cut down the "tree" of guilt that blocks our view of a forgiving and gracious Father every time we remember that we are now in Christ. Christ's righteousness is our righteousness. And amazingly, when God looks down on us, He sees Christ's work on our behalf and not our own!

Key Verses

"They show that the work of the law is written on their hearts, while their conscience also bears witness, and their conflicting thoughts accuse or even excuse them on that day when, according to

my gospel, God judges the secrets of men by Christ Jesus." (Romans 2:15–16)

"But God shows his love for us in that while we were still sinners, Christ died for us. Since, therefore, we have now been justified by his blood, much more shall we be saved by him from the wrath of God. For if, while we were enemies, we were reconciled to God by the death of his Son, much more, now that we are reconciled, shall we be saved by his life." (Romans 5:8–10)

TREE #4 – LONELINESS

One of the saddest human feelings is loneliness or estrangement. Perhaps the people who have experienced the greatest loneliness and estrangement are the more than 30,000 placed in orphanages across Japan. Many were abandoned too early to remember their parents. Others were placed in orphanages after experiencing abuse, hurt, and pain. But orphans are not the only ones who feel loneliness and abandonment.

The elderly are another growing segment of Japanese society experiencing abandonment and loneliness. The combination of an aging society where over 25% is over 65 years of age plus the increasing break down of family force many elderly people to live by themselves with very little interaction with others. The formation of companies like the "rent a family" service where the elderly is temporarily allowed to experience a three-generation family for a day, show how desperate the situation is. Over half a million seniors live alone on state welfare. Their income is often so low they turn to petty crime to fill in the gap. The number of seniors under criminal investigation has tripled from 2001 to 2011 from 5% to 16%!

In addition to orphans and the elderly, the homeless know the shame and sadness of abandonment and loneliness. They are mostly men in their 50s and 60s, day laborers who worked for years without fringe benefits and have nothing, and now are systematically ostracized.

These extreme cases of isolation may seem far removed from our daily lives, but we too have had moments of loneliness, when we feel alone even though there are people around us. Have you asked the question, "Does anyone really care about me?" At such times we feel empty, that something is wrong.

The Bible explains why we feel this way. In Genesis, we learn how our relationship with God has been broken and this broken relationship with God is why we possess a deep sense of abandonment and loneliness. We are created to have a personal relationship with our Creator but instead, we look elsewhere to try to fill the longings of our heart. We feel abandoned, but in reality we have this emptiness because we are the ones who have abandoned God.

Thankfully, God does not leave us with these feelings. We can think of Him as a judge in a court room. He has our case and has pronounced us guilty and worthy of punishment, but then He does something shocking. Instead of pronouncing the punishment, He tells us that it has been paid in full. God, the just judge declares that Jesus has paid the debt and we can go free. Then He does something even more surprising. He gets down from the judge's chair in the court room, comes over to us, puts his arms around us, and says, "From this day on you're my adopted child. I have registered your name under my name. You're to come home with me to live as my own legally adopted child." When we accept God's free gift of forgiveness in Jesus, we are not just forgiven sinners, but we are His sons and daughters. We are His family members. This is how God delivers us from fear of abandonment and loneliness.

As adopted children of God nothing can prevent us from approaching our Heavenly Father. We have access at all times! An illustration of this can be seen with President Kennedy. Even though he was very busy as the President of the United States, he told his staff that his two young children were free to come into the Oval Office any time they wanted. They were not to stop the children from coming. There are pictures in a famous magazine of his son, John Kennedy Jr., crawling underneath the president's desk. His little daughter, Carolyn, is sitting on his lap smiling in pride and delight! This is a picture of the way our Heavenly Father welcomes us to come to Him anytime!

Adoption is difficult to fully grasp in Japan where the adoption of a child without blood relation is unusual. Ninety percent of adoptions in Japan are young men between 20 and 30 years of age. They are adopted as *mukoyoshi* for the purpose of carrying on the family name or business. Adopting young children is much more unusual because the law states that they can be reclaimed for any reason by their birth parents until they are 18. To encourage more adults to adopt young children the government has lowered this age to 16, but it has had little effect.

The stigma attached to adopting a young child is another reason for why few adoptions take place. Adopting parents worry that their child might be teased when found out that they are adopted. Our doctor had to advise a patient who could not have a child to make arrangements to go away for six months and then come back home with her adopted baby. By pretending to have this child while away, she could hide that the baby was not her own and protect her child from possible teasing in the future.

These conditions that exist today in Japan make adoption difficult to be viewed positively. But the Bible teaches that God's adoption of His children is central to the message of the gospel. It is a beautiful picture of God's act of love that will remove our fear and pain of abandonment. The doctrine of adoption has been one of the most ignored doctrines of the church in Japan, but we must make it central to our emotional well-being and security.

When a child is first adopted into a family, it takes a while for that child to feel secure enough in his or her new home to stop fearing return to the orphanage one day. A newly adopted child of God can also feel insecure and act like an orphan, but as we learn to rest on three truths, our fears will turn to confidence. One, it is God who chose us to be adopted. It was not our decision. His decisions are permanent and do not change. Two, we did nothing to influence or persuade God to adopt us. It was not our good character or good efforts that influenced Him. Since our adoption depends totally upon God's gracious decision, there is nothing we can do to change His mind! The laws of Japan make adoption uncertain when it allows the birth parents to take back their child any time until he or she turns 16. The adopted child lives in uncertainty of the future. But this is not the case with God's adoption of us. Three, God's motivation for our adoption is purely based on His love. He loves us so much that in order to make our adoption possible He gave up His own beloved Son, Jesus. The heavenly Father's love is so deep that there is nothing that can remove us from Him. He will be by our side through all of life and safely take us home to live in His presence.

When we feel alone and abandoned, we can remember who adopted us. We belong to God our loving Father. When we believe in our adoption, we are cutting down that "tree" of loneliness and fear of abandonment that blocks our view of the God of grace.

Key Verses

"And because you are sons, God has sent the Spirit of his Son into our hearts, crying, 'Abba! Father!' So you are no longer a slave, but a son, and if a son, then an heir through God." (Galatians 4:6–7)

"For you did not receive the spirit of slavery to fall back into fear, but you have received the Spirit of adoption as sons, by whom we cry, 'Abba! Father!' The Spirit himself bears witness with our spirit that we are children of God, and if children, then heirs—heirs of God and fellow heirs with Christ." (Romans 8:15–17)

"Who shall separate us from the love of Christ? Shall tribulation, or

distress, or persecution, or famine, or nakedness, or danger, or
sword? As it is written, 'For your sake we are being killed all the
day long; we are regarded as sheep to be slaughtered.' No, in all these
things we are more than conquerors through him who loved us. For
I am sure that neither death nor life, nor angels nor rulers, nor
things present nor things to come, nor powers, nor height nor depth,
nor anything else in all creation, will be able to separate us from the
love of God in Christ Jesus our Lord." (Romans 8:35-39)

TREE #5 - DEATH

Feelings of alienation, condemnation, guilt, and loneliness block
our view of the God of grace. However, faith in the work of Jesus
Christ enables us to see this God more clearly. We have been given
the amazing gift of being united with Christ, forgiven, accepted,
and adopted into His family.

His gift for us is truly wonderful, but even though God has
done all this for us, we face a problem. Left to ourselves without
outside help, we will not accept this gift and enjoy a life of fellowship with God. Until God does a powerful work within our hearts
through the work of the Holy Spirit, we will not accept His provision. The Spirit must make us alive before we can accept His gift.

We need to look at the condition of our heart that refuses to
accept His provision of mercy, grace, and love. What God says
about our hearts is not flattering. Paul writes that until God
changes our hearts, we are like dead people unable to act.

"And you were *dead* in the trespasses and sins in which you
once walked, following the course of this world...but God,
being rich in mercy, because of the great love with which he
loved us, even when we were *dead* in our trespasses, made us
alive together with Christ—by grace you have been saved."
(Ephesians 2:1-2, 4-5)

"Dead" is a strong word! A dead body cannot move on its own unless some outside force acts on it.

Jesus tells us that the problem of the Pharisees was their hearts. They were not literally dead but their hearts were closed to accepting Jesus. He says,

> "For this people's heart has grown dull, and with their ears they can barely hear, and their eyes they have closed, lest they should see with their eyes and hear with their ears and understand with their heart and turn, and I would heal them." (Matthew 13:15)

In the Book of Acts, we read an account of how when God works on a heart, the heart will change and believe.

> "And on the Sabbath day we went outside the gate to the riverside, where we supposed there was a place of prayer, and we sat down and spoke to the women who had come together. One who heard us was a woman named Lydia, from the city of Thyatira, a seller of purple goods, who was a worshiper of God. The Lord opened her heart to pay attention to what was said by Paul." (Acts 16:13–14)

When Lydia opened her heart, God brought it to life so she would believe and submit her life to Him.

We must be willing to admit in our own hearts that unless God brings our dead hearts to life, we will not have faith. We will not become His children. It is important to understand, however, the motivation for God to bring us life. It has nothing to do with being good people. It is only because of His grace.

> "For by grace you have been saved through faith. And this is not your own doing; it is the gift of God, not a result of works, so that no one may boast." (Ephesians 2:8–9)

Just think of how amazing this is! The very power that brought Jesus back to life after being dead in the grave for three days is the power that brings us to life. This is why we say that God must first complete this work on our hearts to bring us to life before we become His workmanship.

> "For we are his workmanship, created in Christ Jesus for good works, which God prepared beforehand, that we should walk in them." (Ephesians 2:10)

Does the fact that we are all dead until God brings us to life mean we are all incapable of doing anything good? No, there are many kind people who do good things for others but have no faith in God. Their good deeds help build a healthy society. If one is not motivated to do good deeds for God then what motivates him or her? There are several motivations of the heart, the most appealing of which is to look respectable and to gain a good reputation. And on a personal level, it feels good to do something good. There is a sense of satisfaction. It is reassuring and rewarding. Others are motivated by a belief that doing good will bring a personal reward or good luck from a higher power or deceased ancestors who are looking down on them. All these motivations are self-centered in that they are seeking personal gain rather than desiring to please or thank God. Thus, without a new heart from God, all motivations are driven by a desire to look good in front of others, feel good about oneself, and gain a reward.

It sounds harsh for God to demand we offer up to Him our good works in order to be accepted and get into heaven. But actually, if we had to do good deeds in order to be accepted by God, then we would be faced with the same temptation to look to our efforts as the non-Christians do. Our motivations would turn from wanting to thank God for all He has done for us to the selfish motivations mentioned above. We too would want to look good in front of others, feel good about ourselves through good actions, and bargain with God for blessings through our good efforts.

When God brought us from death to life, we were changed and stopped striving to be good in order to be accepted by God. Instead of striving to be blessed, we now depend on what God has done for us in His Son, Jesus Christ. Since He obeyed all the laws for us, we are made righteous as a free gift. This moves our hearts and makes us thankful and desirous to love and live for God. Our motivation is not to get something from God but to give Him our love and to obey Him out of gratitude.

The moment we are brought to life by God we experience regeneration. What does the regenerated life look like? It is a life that starts with a new heart given to Him enabling us to love God and grieve over sin. To the regenerated person repentance is no longer something to be feared. It is not an enemy to be avoided, but a way of repeatedly experiencing the forgiving arms of the Father who always welcomes us back. This love received from the Father makes us take sin seriously knowing the great cost of the death of Jesus.

Death is no longer a "tree" that keeps us from seeing the glory of the God of grace, who shines beautifully like Mt. Fuji in the clear blue sky. The Bible says we don't see him because we were dead. God had to do the work of regeneration to bring us to life and enable us to see His beauty.

Key Verse

"And you were dead in the trespasses and sins in which you once walked, following the course of this world, following the prince of the power of the air, the spirit that is now at work in the sons of disobedience—among whom we all once lived in the passions of our flesh, carrying out the desires of the body and the mind, and were by nature children of wrath, like the rest of mankind. But God, being rich in mercy, because of the great love with which he loved us,

*even when we were dead in our trespasses, made us alive together
with Christ—by grace you have been saved—and raised us up with
him and seated us with him in the heavenly places in Christ Jesus,
so that in the coming ages he might show the immeasurable riches of
his grace in kindness toward us in Christ Jesus. For by grace you
have been saved through faith. And this is not your own doing; it is
the gift of God, not a result of works, so that no one may boast. For
we are his workmanship, created in Christ Jesus for good works,
which God prepared beforehand, that we should walk in them.”*
(Ephesians 2:1–10)

TREE #6 - HOPELESSNESS

God changes our hearts when we become His children, and
through the work of the Holy Spirit, we desire to obey Him.
Before we were not aware of our disobedience to God, but now we
are. Not knowing God, it was as though we were swimming down-
stream. Now that we are called to put our selfish life aside and
obey God, we are doing the difficult task of swimming upstream.
And when we try to swim without dependence on what God has
done for us, we become discouraged and think that the Christian
life is hopelessly difficult. In our discouragement, God seems
distant and unconcerned. Feelings of hopelessness become another
“tree” that blocks our view of God.

When we face discouragement from the lack of ability to be
faithful to God, He provides something to encourage us. He
provides a space where we can stumble and fail but still be safe. It
is similar to the life of the salmon that hatches from an egg in a
cool, clean, and safe spring that can grow strong enough to venture
out into the dangerous ocean. Where is the safe place God places
us so we will be safe as new Christians? This safe place is a life in
Christ.

“And you, who were dead in your trespasses and the uncircumcision of your flesh, God made alive together with him, having forgiven us all our trespasses, by canceling the record of debt that stood against us with its legal demands. This he set aside, nailing it to the cross." (Colossians 2:13–14)

This is a safe place because when we are in Christ we are forgiven and our sins are cancelled. God deals with our failures by canceling them. We are encouraged to know that God forgives and forgets our sins by nailing them to the cross. Without the promise of the cross, we would feel hopelessly bound in our sins.

We are safe as God's children because He pursues us and brings us back when we wander away. There is a story about a father, son, and toy sailboat that illustrates our Father's persistent love. With the help of his father, a young boy built a beautiful toy sailboat. He was very proud of this boat and eager to sail it on the lake. Due to strong winds, the boat was pulled so hard that the string attached to it broke, and it was blown out of sight. After looking in vain for the boat, he sadly went home. The next day, the boy walked past a pawn shop. To his amazement, there in the window sat the sailboat he and his father had built. He rushed into the store and told the man that the boat in the window was his. The store owner said he could have it back, but first he would have to pay $20. The boy ran home, told his mother, took his own money, and bought back the boat. The boy had made the boat, it was his, but he had to pay the pawn shop owner to buy it back. This is a picture of what our Heavenly Father did for us. God made us and we belong to Him but in disobedience we wandered away. God chose to buy us back again at great expense. The price that our Father paid to buy us back was the price of the death of His son on the cross.

God's act of buying us back not only makes us secure but also makes us humble. Along with Paul we must say, "Far be it from me to boast except in the cross of our Lord Jesus Christ, by which the world has been crucified to me, and I to the world" (Galatians

6:14). We are humbled to know that we are no more able to return back to God on our own than the boy's toy sailboat. Motivated purely out of love and mercy, God brings us back to Him.

When God changes our hearts, we are able to appreciate the tremendous debt He paid on the cross to make us His children. The Holy Spirit gives us the assurance to rest in the gift of Christ and enables us to swim upstream against the current. Swimming against the current is what we do when we follow Christ. We fight against the nature of our hearts that fight against yielding our will to God. Knowing how much He has paid to bring us back creates in our hearts the desire to love and worship Him.

This new desire to love and worship God is the new power that works within us to make the outcome of our journey radically different from the salmon returning to Hokkaido. Only 1–3% of the hundreds of millions of salmon released from hatcheries every year in Hokkaido actually survive to return home. We, on the other hand, are not like salmon in the dangerous sea. We have been given the guarantee of assurance as His children. His guarantee provides protection for those who are in Christ from start to finish. He chose us, forgives us, and justifies us by paying the penalty for sin through His Son's death on the cross. He adopts us as His children, makes us alive in Christ in order to change us to be more like Him, and brings us safely to our real home of glory. Remembering this removes all feelings of hopelessness, removing yet another "tree" that blocks our view of the God of grace.

Key Verses

> *"For by him all things were created, in heaven and on earth, visible and invisible, whether thrones or dominions or rulers or authorities —all things were created through him and for him. And he is before all things, and in him all things hold together. And he is the head of the body, the church. He is the beginning, the firstborn from the dead, that in everything he might be preeminent. For in him all*

*the fullness of God was pleased to dwell, and through him to recon-
cile to himself all things, whether on earth or in heaven, making
peace by the blood of his cross." (Colossians 1:16–20)*

*"For I am sure that neither death nor life, nor angels nor rulers, nor
things present nor things to come, nor powers, nor height nor depth,
nor anything else in all creation, will be able to separate us from the
love of God in Christ Jesus our Lord." (Romans 8:38–39)*

TREE #7 – FEELINGS OF INADEQUACY

The seventh tree is feelings of not measuring up and lacking confidence in ourselves. God's desire for His children is to conform
them into the image of Christ. This is a high calling and one that is
impossible to fully reach in this life. But when we understand that
God is committed to helping us, our attitude changes from feelings of inadequacy and guilt to hope. We come to a greater appreciation of God's grace. We will consider three ways (justification,
sanctification, glorification) that God works salvation in our lives
and then observe how God is committed to accomplishing this.

Our Goal

"And we know that for those who love God all things work
together for good, for those who are called according to his
purpose. For those whom he foreknew he also predestined
to be *conformed* to the image of his Son, in order that he
might be the firstborn among many brothers." (Romans
8:28–29)

The Greek Paul uses to describe the process of being
conformed to Christ's image is *summorphos*. This is the root word
for "metamorphose" in modern English. It refers to the change a
caterpillar goes through in a cocoon in order to become a beautiful

butterfly. Paul uses *summorphos* to refer to the process God uses to turn us into the image of the most beautiful, loving, and sinless person who ever lived, Jesus Christ.

In this process of transformation, we are not passive but active participants with God.

> "Therefore, my beloved, as you have always obeyed, so now, not only as in my presence but much more in my absence work out your own salvation (*"soteria"*) with fear and trembling, for it is God who works in you, both to will and to work for his good pleasure." (Philippians 2:12–13)

The Greek word *soteria* ("salvation") refers to three conditions of our life in Christ: justification, sanctification, and glorification. We begin our journey when we confess our sins and accept Jesus into our hearts. This is called justification, declared righteous in Christ. Paul uses this word in Romans 1:16,

> "I am not ashamed of the gospel, for it is the power of God for salvation (*"soteria"*) to everyone who believes, to the Jew first and also to the Greek."

Our justification is a once-for-all declaration of God over those who come to Christ in repentance and faith. He declares, "You are saved."

After being declared righteous in Christ, God continues His work of sanctification by changing us to live more Christ-like lives. The verb Paul uses to describe this work is the same root word *"soteria"* in its present, continuing tense. He continues his work of "salvation" every day of our life in Christ, and we refer to this process as sanctification.

When we die and are with the Lord, we are saved by being made holy and free from all sin. Once again, Paul uses the same root word "*soteria*," but in this case he uses it in the future tense to refer to our glorification or our "glorified" state in heaven.

> "Therefore, I endure everything for the sake of the elect,
> that they also may obtain the salvation *("soteria")* that is in
> Christ Jesus with eternal glory." (2 Timothy 2:10)

In Christ, we have been saved in the past (justification), we are being saved in the present (sanctification), and we will be saved in the future (glorification).

It is inconsistent to Paul's message to interpret the words, "work out your own salvation (*"soteria"*) with fear and trembling," as justification. In this verse, he refers to *soteria* as our sanctification. God works gradual changes as we live diligent and disciplined lives of fellowship and obedience to Christ. We are called to be diligent, but we are not on our own. In the same verse, he assures us, "God works in you, both to will and to work for his pleasure." Knowing God will help us is the encouragement we need to work earnestly towards our sanctification. The way God works is to first change our hearts so we desire to become more like Christ, and then he gives us the strength to not be stuck in our old selfish ways.

Later in Chapter 3, we will consider how God brings change in our lives through His Holy Spirit, His Word, and the fellowship of Christians and the church. All these are gifts that enable us to be transformed into the beautiful butterfly like the image of Christ Jesus.

Do we really believe the gospel?

God provides for all our needs, but do we really rest in what He has done? In His kindness and grace, God helps us overcome our shame, fear, guilt, loneliness, and hopelessness. He accomplished this through his Son. Jesus came and lived the perfect life, died as punishment for our sins in our stead because God in His holiness hates sin and must punish sin with death. When we grab hold of this wonderful gospel message it changes the way we look at our sin because we are defined by His righteousness and not by our poor selfish attempts to be good. This enables us to see God as holy and hate sin. Rather than being afraid, we can boldly approach Him as forgiven and loved children. Confidence and humility are signs that we truly understand and trust in the gospel. Guilt and shame from failure are replaced by assurance in His acceptance, and we live in gratitude, worship, and peace.

Do we really live in the gospel? Is the gospel message the road we walk every day? The true test is to ask, "Am I living a life of repentance and faith? Do I see that Christ is my righteousness and in him I am forgiven, and my sins don't condemn me anymore?" If we can say "Yes" to these questions, we have the gift of a new identity. We are the righteous ones in Christ. This is what helps us deal with shame, fear, loneliness, and struggles. It is what gives the boldness and assurance to grow in our relationship with our God of grace. It does not mean we never face fear and are tempted to live under the bondage of guilt. But when we are tempted, we are given this powerful assurance. God's acceptance and forgiveness defines who we are as His loved and righteous children. The confidence and humility we gain from this identity in Christ brings change to our lives. It frees us from feelings of inadequacy, another "tree" that blocks our view, and keeps the God of grace clearly in sight.

Key Verse

"Therefore, my beloved, as you have always obeyed, so now, not only as in my presence but much more in my absence work out your own salvation ("soteria") with fear and trembling, for it is God who works in you, both to will and to work for his good pleasure." (Philippians 2:12–13)

TREE #8 – SEPARATION

The third and final stage of our salvation is glorification. This future promise should give much hope. We should be changing and growing but when we see we are not, we struggle with a guilty conscience. We may understand in theory that God is committed to our growth but like the very small number of 1–3% of salmon that return to their home successfully, we fear we too may be separated from God and not make it home due to the many dangers surrounding us. We wonder to ourselves if we will really reach that future stage of glorification. This fear is the eighth tree, preventing us from seeing the God of grace.

There is, however, an enormous difference between the salmon surviving in the ocean, and we who are living as children of God. The difference is God's commitment to us. We live under His care, and He offers us a guarantee. He says that none of us will be destroyed by the world's dangers. He promises to take us through life safely until we see Him face to face in the new world. Not 3% but 100% will be brought home safely. The work He has begun will be completed in glory. We will never be separated from the presence of God.

"I am sure of this, that he who began a good work in you
will bring it to completion at the day of Jesus Christ."
(Philippians 1:6)

Jesus assures us with these words.

"I give them eternal life, and they will never perish, and no
one will snatch them out of my hand. My Father, who has
given them to me, is greater than all, and no one is able to
snatch them out of the Father's hand." (John 10:28–29)

What enables us to believe God will bring us home safely to

heaven? Our confidence is not placed on how faithful we think we have been. Most Christians feel like they have failed repeatedly in their attempt to live for Christ, so this cannot be the basis of our confidence. No, our only confidence is placed upon what Christ has already done for us. It is based only upon the work, death, and resurrection of Jesus Christ. He said He would be resurrected and since He was, we can believe that He will also return to earth. When He does, all evil on earth will be done away with. All the wrong things on earth will be ended and we will be with Christ as sinless people who are fully able to praise God. It also means that we will receive glorified bodies far superior to what we have now.

"So it is with the resurrection of the dead. What is sown is perishable; what is raised is imperishable. It is sown in dishonor; it is raised in glory. It is sown in weakness; it is raised in power. It is sown a natural body; it is raised a spiritual body." (I Corinthians 15:42-44)

It is helpful to put the promise of our glorification in the larger picture of God's plan for history, which can be seen in four stages.

1. Creation — God first created the world free from sin.
2. Fall — The perfect became imperfect when mankind went his own way and disobeyed God.
3. Redemption — The world has been groaning since the fall of man. In God's mercy and kindness, He did not leave us to our own destruction but sent His Son.
4. Restoration — The new heavens and new earth begin.

The story is not complete with creation–fall–redemption. It must also include the fourth stage—the restoration of the world. God created the heavens and the earth perfectly, but with man's disobedience the world suffered decay and harm. When Christ returns again, He will not just restore the world to its perfect pre-fallen state, but to a different, even more glorified state. At that time, the prayer that the Lord taught us to pray, "Thy will be done on earth as it is in Heaven," will be fully answered. The new heavens and new earth will begin with the return of Jesus Christ in glory.

At the creation of the world, sin did not exist. At the fall, man became a slave to sin. He was unable not to sin. With our redemption in Christ, it has become possible not to sin, but in the final restoration of heaven and earth, it will not be possible to sin any longer. Sin will be gone from us forever.

It is this hope that enables us to face overwhelming discouragements and suffering that comes from pain, sorrow, and injustice. These too can block our view of the God of grace. When we focus our hopes on God's plan for the future where all things wrong will be made right, it will sustain us through this life. When we do, we will be able to look forward to experiencing God in a new and fuller way. Our view of Him will never again be blocked by "trees" along the road.

This hope in future glorification has radically changed the lives of many. Nikolaus Zinzendorf was a count in Germany who gave away his wealth and prestige in order to begin the first missionary movement in the Western church. His devotion started this movement in the 1760s. He wrote,

"Remember, you must never use your position to lord it over the heathen. Instead, you must humble yourself and earn their respect through your own quiet faith and the power of the Holy Spirit. The missionary must seek nothing for himself, no seat of honor or hope of fame. Like the cab horse in London, each of you must wear blinkers that blind you to every danger and to every snare and conceit. You must be content to suffer, to die, and to be forgotten."[2]

We can suffer, die, and be forgotten because God will never forget us. Our hope is in God who will provide an eternal home with Him.

Key Verse

"Then I saw a new heaven and a new earth, for the first heaven and the first earth had passed away, and the sea was no more. And I saw the holy city, new Jerusalem, coming down out of heaven from God, prepared as a bride adorned for her husband. And I heard a loud voice from the throne saying, 'Behold, the dwelling place of God is with man. He will dwell with them, and they will be his people, and God himself will be with them as their God. He will wipe away every tear from their eyes, and death shall be no more, neither shall there be mourning, nor crying, nor pain anymore, for the former things have passed away.'" (Revelation 21:1–4)

CHAPTER 3

HOW ARE WE CHANGED WHEN WE LOOK AT GOD?

Something special happens when we stop to look at Mt. Fuji. We relax and feel emotionally refreshed. Our blood pressure goes down. Mt. Fuji is only a mountain that has no power to change us, but this is not the case when we stop to look and meditate on God and Jesus Christ. Far more than relaxing, looking to God changes us. Our hearts are affected. We are enabled to love God and others.

In the previous chapter, we outlined obstacles, various "trees" that block our view of the God of grace. Now we need to consider how God has made it possible to see Him more fully. And when we do, how does God change us?

We do not have the right to look at God, for He is holy and we are not. The privilege we have today was not available to people thousands of years ago. They had to be careful about how they called on God and were prevented from entering the holy place in the temple. But today, as believers cleansed and made holy by Jesus, we have the right to approach God boldly as His adopted children and call Him "Abba" or "Papa."

CREATION

What has God provided to see Him? Paul tells us we can see God through His creation.

> "For his invisible attributes, namely, his eternal power and divine nature, have been clearly perceived, ever since the creation of the world, in the things that have been made. So they are without excuse." (Romans 1:20)

Israel is reminded to look to the hills to see their Creator.

> "I lift my eyes to the hills. From where does my help come? My help comes from the Lord, who made heaven and earth." (Psalm 121:1–2)

The unlimited number of stars in the sky reminds the Psalmist of the infinite nature of God.

> "He determines the number of the stars; he gives to all of them their names. Great is our Lord, and abundant in power; his understanding is beyond measure." (Psalm 147:4–5)

The moon and the stars remind him of God's love.

> "The moon and stars to rule over the night, for his steadfast love endures forever." (Psalm 136:9)

David declares that the universe speaks to us as if God himself was speaking.

> "The heavens declare the glory of God, and the sky above

proclaims his handiwork. Day to day pours out speech, and night to night reveals knowledge." (Psalm 19:1–2)

We live in a modern world with artificial lighting, concrete pavement, and tall buildings that make it harder to see the stars and observe the clear sky. When I stood in the Negev several miles south of Bethlehem in the darkness of the night as the shepherd David did years before, I was amazed to see so many stars. In the crystal-clear air, they seemed within my reach. We can see why the Psalmist was so impressed. It convinced him of the Creator's power.

WORD OF GOD

Creation is God's general revelation, but He has provided more specific revelation in the Word of God, which tells us everything we need to know about who God is. Through the Bible's message, we not only learn about Him in a general way, but we also know Him in a personal way. Using men like Moses, David, and others, He guided them to write down what He wanted us to know in such a way that the content is without mistake. We can read it and believe every sentence and statement as infallible. We do not need to discard any part of it, nor do we need to add to it. It is complete and perfect. It must be utterly reliable because our fallen nature wants to believe what is appealing to us and avoid believing that which we dislike.

The Word of God as found in the Bible corrects selfish desires, challenging or convincing us to change, preventing us from picking and choosing texts that support our thinking while ignoring others. When discouraged, it assures us of the promises of God, who still loves us despite our failures. Because the Bible is God's Word and without mistake, we can believe that we are forgiven and accepted even when we do not feel like it. God has given a trustworthy text that provides an accurate picture of who He is. We can humbly accept His promises and submit.

God gave the Bible to read regularly to protect and shape the affections of our hearts. The Psalmist says the Bible is our protection.

"I have stored up your word in my heart that I might not sin against you." (Psalm 119:11)

And the Bible is central to everyday life.

"His delight is in the law of the Lord, and on his law he meditates day and night." (Psalm 1:2)

It is medicine to our sad and lonely hearts.

"The Lord is gracious and merciful, slow to anger and abounding in steadfast love. The Lord is good to all, and his mercy is over all that he has made." (Psalm 145:8–9)

And it gives a message to pass on to our children.

"One generation shall commend your works to another, and shall declare your mighty acts. . . . They shall pour forth the fame of your abundant goodness and shall sing aloud of your righteousness." (Psalm 145:4, 7)

JESUS CHRIST

Jesus Christ is the ultimate way we can see God with clarity. Jesus said about Himself, "I and the Father are one" (John 10:30) and "He who has seen Me has seen the Father!" (John 14:9). Every word He spoke, every attitude He had, and every action He took was the perfect reflection of the character of God the Father. He is

Immanuel, God with us. Because Jesus came to earth as a human for over thirty years, teaching and showing who God is, we know the answer to these important questions:

Why do we believe God forgives sinners?

> *We know how God feels about sinners by looking at how Jesus welcomed sinners and forgave them.*

Why do we know that God hates and punishes sin?

> *We see how much He hates sin by requiring His own Son to die on the cross as punishment.*

Why do we know that God is eternal and will return once again to earth to re-establish a new heaven and earth for all His children?

> *Because Jesus died and was resurrected to life, we can believe that He will return as promised. He suffered and experienced every temptation and hardship, so we can see the heart of God towards those who suffer. He understands our trials. In all these ways, He is the perfect image of God. Jesus is the reason we can know that God is personal and not some impersonal force.*

THE HOLY SPIRIT

God provided someone who lives in us to enable us to experience Him more personally, the Holy Spirit. With the help of the Spirit, we can see God with the eyes of our hearts. His task is to help us understand and remember what Jesus said.

> "The Helper, the Holy Spirit, whom the Father will send in my name, he will teach you all things and bring to your remembrance all that I have said to you." (John 14:26)

The Spirit will not just help us remember Jesus's teaching but assure us of how special we are to God.

> "I will ask the Father and he will give you another Helper, to be with you forever, even the Spirit of truth, whom the world cannot receive because it neither sees him nor knows him. You know him, for he dwells with you and will be in you. I will not leave you as orphans; I will come to you."
> (John 14:16–18)

What could be more amazing and reassuring than to have our heavenly Father constantly live with us through His Spirit! The Spirit is what makes it possible to feel Him intimately in our hearts rather than just look at Him from a distance.

BODY OF CHRIST

There is yet another help to see our God of grace more clearly. Humans are created to be social. The body of Christ experienced through the community of believers adds another dimension to seeing God.

The love Jesus displayed on earth is a perfect picture of what a Christian community looks like. To be Christ-like, this community should be characterized by humility, sensitivity, and acceptance of all people, both the good and unlikeable. When Christian community acts this way toward each other, its members experience God's love and forgiveness. What motivates this love to be present in such a community is realizing that each person is guilty of being a sinner and yet has been forgiven, loved, and accepted in Christ. Experiencing the patient, loving heart of God in Jesus shapes our hearts so we can treat others the same way. When Christian community lives out of humility and confidence in Christ, it makes it possible for people to see and experience the grace of God.

Being in this community is an important part of growth in our walk with Christ. We are given a new identity in Christ, but we are also given identity as part of the body of Christ as a new family. This is where we grow in our understanding and love for God. It is our honor and privilege to belong to this new family.

The gospel is not a message to each person apart from family. When we take advantage of living in this new community with other brothers and sisters in the Lord, something special happens. It is similar to viewing a beautiful mountain or piece of art. Our instinct is to share it with others. Sharing this experience with someone makes it more special and meaningful. Our experiences of God take on deeper meaning when we share them in community, enabling us to grow in knowledge and grace.

KNOW GOD IS ALWAYS VISIBLE

There is a big difference between how we see Mt. Fuji through the seasons of the year and how we daily experience the God of grace. Even though Mt. Fuji rises over 12,000 ft from the land around it with no other mountains to block it, it is not always visible. From November to January, it is visible 80% of the time, but for the rest of the year it is hidden from view. To get a glimpse, you have to get up early in the morning or wait until sunset or wait until after a typhoon when the wind has cleared the air. Because of rain, overcast clouds, haze, and smog during the months of June through August, Mt. Fuji is visible only 10% of the time.

However, this is not the case with God. He has given glasses to make it possible to see Him daily in every situation of life. Thanks be to God that we never have to lose sight of Him because of His provision through nature, Scripture, Jesus Christ, the Holy Spirit, and Christian community. They are the lenses He has given to see Him daily.

BECOME LIKE CHRIST

When we look to the God of grace something special happens. We are changed to become more like Christ. This change begins as we hear the beautiful music of the message. Before, we may have heard individual notes but failed to hear the music. It is only when we hear the music of the gospel that our hearts are affected. It may be true that through determination and strong willpower we can change our behavior, but we cannot change our heart affections through our willpower. Our hearts are changed as we are overwhelmed with the love of God for us.

The theme of God's love is the music we must hear to be changed from the inside out. God does not want us to just try to control our behavior but to obey Him out of love. It is our hearts that God seeks to transform, and therefore He tells us that the greatest commandment is to love God with our heart, soul, and mind. This is also why Paul writes that even though we may give all our things away, even our very lives, if we are not motivated out of love for God, it means nothing (I Corinthians 13:3). Some would say that it doesn't matter what your motivation is, just as long as you do the right thing. Paul's answer to this is that your heart, your attitude, is what God looks at. He wants our love for Him, not just our efforts to obey.

If the gospel is the melody that changes our hearts, we need to learn to recognize it and play it regularly. What is this melody? It is the theme that runs from the beginning of Scripture and plays to the very last chapter. The melody is the story of how God delivers us from evil and freely gives a new life where we can have a relationship with Him as His forgiven, adopted, and cherished children. The story is accomplished by the work of the hero of all the stories in the Bible, Jesus.

Every story in both the Old and New Testament ultimately points to Jesus. The hero of the story does for us what we cannot do for ourselves. We must admit our inability to earn righteousness and receive it from God by accepting Jesus's work on our behalf. By faith, we humbly receive His forgiveness and acceptance. We never outlive our need for the faith that helps us acknowledge that we are big sinners who are loved and forgiven by an even larger love through the grace of God. Faith in God's gift of grace is what will change our hearts. What saved and changed us on our first day is the same faith that continues to change us daily until the end when we arrive safely at our real home.

CHANGED FROM THE HEART

When God's Word talks about change in our lives, it is not just referring to a change of behavior but a change of heart. Ordinarily, we don't hear much talk about attitudes or motivations. The focus is more on behavior. This emphasis on behavior is driven by confidence that we can change what we do if we try hard enough.

This thinking brings self-confidence, and it feels good and looks good. Our prideful hearts deceive us by convincing us that with willpower, we can live on our own. When we do not measure up to our own expectations, we look around to find someone worse than ourselves to feel good. This explains why we are always comparing ourselves to others.

The gospel gives a new and better motivation to love and serve God and others. This new, superior motivation comes from a changed heart that is no longer focused on oneself but God. It is a new heart that desires to live for God and extend to others the same love and grace he or she has received from God. This heart is filled with the assurance of God's love to not need the approval of others. This new heart frees us from the fear of others. It also frees us from the fear of failure. God is not a hard taskmaster but is kind, patient, and forgiving of our sins since Christ paid for those sins.

The motivations that affect our hearts make a tremendous difference in how we carry out our jobs. Pastor Tim Keller shares a story of two women who were both hired to do the same job. They were hired to work in a small room with no windows. Both worked under the same conditions but one woman was told that she would receive a salary of one hundred dollars, and the other woman, ten thousand dollars. The woman with the smaller wage complained how tiresome her job was, but the other, anticipating ten thousand dollars, kept working with a good attitude.[1]

It is a lot easier to put up with hardship, boredom, and have a good attitude toward our tasks when we have strong motivation. While Christians are not rewarded with money, they have received something of even greater worth, the invaluable gift of God's love, acceptance, and eternal reward after life on earth. Those who have not received this gift are left with the alternative of working hard to gain acceptance and success, never knowing if they have done enough. It can be an exhausting way to live.

SEE THE BEAUTY OF THE MUSIC

In order to hear the music of the gospel, we need to see the difference between religion and the message of the gospel. These contrasts, outlined in many of Tim Keller's books and sermons, illustrate the difference between looking to one's own goodness and looking to God to grace us with His gift.

- In religion, you obey to be accepted. In the gospel, you are accepted and therefore obey.
- In religion, motivation is based on fear and insecurity. In the gospel, motivation is driven by a grateful, joyous heart committed to obeying God and keeping Him first.
- In religion, you obey to get things. In the gospel, you obey to delight in God and resemble Him.
- In religion, when things do not go your way, you get angry thinking you deserve better. In the gospel, you suffer when things go wrong, but you are assured that

the Father loves you and will always be there in the midst of trials and hardship.

- In religion, when you are criticized or ostracized, you become outraged because it is important to think of yourself as a good person. Threats to your self-image must be prevented at all costs. In the gospel, when you are criticized, it is painful, but your self-image does not depend on what others think of you as a good person. Your identity is not built on the opinions of others but on what Christ thinks of you and on God's love for you.

- In religion, your prayer life is very narrow in scope; it consists primarily of requests, which become more intense when you are in need. In the gospel, your prayer life is mainly about praise and adoration. It is about maintaining a close relationship of fellowship with God.

- In religion, your self-view swings between two poles. When you live up to your standards, you feel confident but tend to become proud and unsympathetic. When you do not measure up to your own standards, you lose confidence and feel like a failure. But in the gospel, you know yourself to be an even bigger sinner than you realize. And this makes you humble. At the same time, you know that God has forgiven you in Jesus Christ, so you can be confident in His love and acceptance. You are also sympathetic to other's struggles because you are aware of your own.

HEAR WITH THE HEART

These contrasts between religion and Christianity demonstrate the power of the gospel to change the heart from seeking self-dependence, control, and power. They show how Christians become dependent and obey from a grateful and worshipping heart.

In the country of Japan where external compliance to a set of rules is taught by parents, schools, the government and its religions, it is all the more important that we look below the surface to discover heart motivations that make us so dutifully compliant. Examining our hearts will help us understand the importance of doing things out of love and not duty.

EXAMINE WHAT WE LOVE

Have you ever thought this way? You are what you love. In other words, your behavior is determined by the things you long for and consider important to you. They are the things that you feel you must have to be happy, daydream about, long for, and work towards. They determine how you spend your time and money.

When it comes to motivating people to behave in a certain way, we treat them as though they are primarily a brain that needs to take in information. We neglect the fact that they have a heart and this is what ultimately controls what they do. Human beings are primarily motivated by heart desires, but instead, we appeal to others with instructions and rules to follow. We think that by giving information on how to act responsibly, they will comply and feel good when they do. And if this does not work, then we turn to pressure. The threat of criticism, isolation, rejection, and shame are effective tools to control behavior. But while they may change behavior, they do not change what God is primarily concerned about, the heart. In Chapter 2, we observed the old lady sitting in judgment of the young girl putting on makeup on the train. She is an example of how focus on external behaviors grows a judgmental heart.

There are some who say it is enough to keep the rules even though the motivations are wrong. Since the focus is on compliant behavior this explains why there is little talk about motivations. The compliant person is respected and praised. But in reality, motivations have an important effect on our attitudes toward others. If we are motivated out of fear of rejection or criticism, we will be threatened by relationships. If we are motivated out of pride, when others do not measure up to our standards, we become harsh and critical. While there is nothing wrong with being a good member of a group or polite and sensitive to the needs of others, doing so out of selfish reasons can lead to holding resentments and growing a judgmental heart.

But the heart that grasps the gospel of grace will be changed. To emphasize the importance of possessing gospel characteristics mentioned above, I will restate them:

- You are accepted and therefore obey
- Your motivation is driven by a grateful, joyous heart
- You obey God to please Him and resemble Him
- Your self-image does not depend on others thinking of you as a good person
- Your identity is not built on the opinions of others but on what Christ thinks of you and God's love for you
- Your prayer life is mainly about praise and adoration, about maintaining a close relationship of fellowship with God
- You know yourself to be a big sinner even more than you realize, and this makes you humble. At the same time, you know that God has forgiven you in Jesus Christ, so you can be confident in His love and acceptance.

If what we love shapes what we do and who we become, we must look inside the heart to determine what we love. This is not easy to do, because as the Bible tells us, our hearts deceive us.

"The heart is deceitful above all things, and desperately sick; who can understand it?" (Jeremiah 17:9)

The human heart seeks certain things to feel significant and fulfilled. When we understand what these things are, we can identify what we are looking to to fulfill our hearts. Here is a list of the four basic desires that have a strong influence on what we desire. By asking ourselves the following questions, we can unmask what our heart is seeking. They help us look below the surface and see what is really motivating us.

- Comfort — What do I think will bring me comfort?
  What will give me pleasure or a good quality of life?
- Control — What situation will give me control over my
  life? Do I have enough money, good health, or a
  secure job?
- Power — What will give me a sense of power? Do I
  need people to depend on me to feel important?
- Approval — Do I have the approval of others? Do
  people like me and think I am a good person?[2]

When these desires are threatened, we experience emotions that help identify what our hearts long for. They are surface emotions and thus more identifiable than those below the surface like the desire for comfort, control, power, and approval. Surface emotions such as anger, jealousy, boredom, worry, and discouragement can be used as a tool for self-examination. They can be used as a yellow flag to warn us of some idol below the surface.

Tim Keller used an illustration of how the surface emotion of anger reveals what is happening in the hearts of two mothers. Both were very committed to get their sons into good colleges and were zealous to do all they could. Their husbands, however, were not as committed. Both wives were very angry with their husbands and grew cold towards them. In their frustration, they went separately to talk with the pastor, hoping for change in the lack of involvement of their husbands. The pastor determined the source of the two mothers' anger. In listening to their story, he knew the husbands were not the issue but the desire to see their sons get into a high-level college. The pastor could have encouraged them to forgive their husbands, but this would not address the mothers' real issue. Instead he explained to the two mothers the anger came from an ultimate goal that was being blocked. One mother came to see how her son had become an idol, and this was the source of her anger and resentment toward her husband. When she admitted that her son's success had become an idol, the resentment lessened, and she could forgive her husband. The other mother resisted and was unwilling to examine her heart and saw the fault being only with her husband and so remained harsh and angry. She would not admit why it was so important that her son succeed. His success meant that she would be respected by others and secure in a more financially certain future. She was unwilling to let go of this and replace it with trust in God.

The pastor could have lectured the two women not to put so much value in their sons' success, but in doing so, he would not have helped the mothers see the real issue. They were using their sons as a way to fulfill their idols instead of turning to Christ to fill their longings. Instead of saying, "God, I am sorry for my anger!" they were forced to see the deeper issue than just anger. Their anger was driven by the idols of recognition and comfort and security. Therefore, a more meaningful prayer of repentance would have been, "Lord, I'm looking to my son's achievement to gain significance and security instead of resting in your love and care for me. Forgive me for putting my trust in these things instead of you. Help me to be content with your love and trust that you will take care of me."

When we pray in this way, we identify our idols and can repent for looking to something besides the Lord to fill our hearts. When we examine our actions and attitudes by looking at the way we react on a surface level, real change will happen. The Spirit takes our effort to identify our idols and convinces us of the sufficiency of Christ's love. This will make us thankful and willing to trust in God. When we take the intentional step to place our heart affections on Him, we are no longer content with lesser things. We will be shaped and molded as people who reflect the likeness of Christ, content to put God first.

WORSHIP OUT OF LOVE

Moses affirms what we have been saying with the following words.

> "You shall love the Lord your God with all your heart and with all your soul and with all your might. And these words that I command you today shall be on your heart."
> (Deuteronomy 6:5–6)

What do we do to have His commands on our hearts? Worshipful contemplation on who God is and His love for us moves our hearts to love Him. It is not enough to read the Bible. The religious leaders were an example of those who studied but declined to examine their hearts. Jesus scolded them for diligently studying God's word but with cold hearts. In their pride, they thought of themselves as not needing forgiveness, and they missed the message of God's love and grace. They attempted to show love of God by reading and memorizing. This emphasis on showing love through their diligent efforts created a proud, judgmental spirit that found fault with everyone, including Jesus. When we follow the commands of Moses to have the Word on our hearts, we will use the Bible to guide us in our worship of Him and our prayers. This will make us thankful and confident in God's love and humble and loving towards others.

These same teachers also taught that we sin because of external contamination. This is why they emphasized the importance of washing hands and not touching unclean things. But Jesus showed that evil comes from our hearts, from within us and not outside.

"For from within, out of the heart of man, come evil

thoughts, sexual immorality, theft, murder, adultery, covet-
ing, wickedness, deceit, sensuality, envy, slander, pride, fool-
ishness. All these evil things come from within, and they
defile a person." (Mark 7:21–23)

We do evil because our hearts deceive us into thinking that our
way is more satisfying than putting God first.

Japanese society does not agree with Jesus's teaching that evil
comes from within. You only need to go to a Shinto shrine to see
this, where people sip from cups of water, rinse out their mouths,
and spit the water back out to symbolize cleansing and getting rid
of evil.

This emphasis on external influence is why we hear so little
about the importance of examining one's heart. Instead, the
emphasis is placed on controlling one's external world through
self-control. Through discipline, we can control our actions. For
example, if a man is addicted to pornography, he is encouraged to
replace this with healthy friendships or devotion to a good hobby.
But there is no discussion of what is causing this addiction. What
is he really seeking when he looks at pornography? The underlying
reason may be driven out of a desire for intimacy with another
person, but he may lack self-confidence. He may be too shy or
timid about developing normal relationships, or he may be too lazy
and selfish to do the hard work of building a relationship. But in
either case, until he believes his emotional need for intimacy is
ultimately driven out of a need for God, he will not become
healthy enough to have a meaningful relationship with a woman.
To really be helped, he needs to look to God to fill the emptiness
he senses instead of looking to something else to fill it. Otherwise,
after overcoming pornography, he will move on to find something
else to fill the emptiness in his life.

The strong emphasis on keeping external rules has positive
results. Unfortunately, the orderliness, safety, and predictability
that Japan possesses have convinced people that rule-keeping is

the answer to problems. For example, note how the Japanese population follows traffic rules. There are few countries like Japan where pedestrians stop and wait for the red light even though no cars are coming and it is the middle of the night! This has made Japan a well-organized country where it is safe to walk on the streets.

Does external compliance to rule-keeping produce a nation of happy people? According to a recent study done by the Organization for Economic Co-operation and Development (OECD), discipline, hard work, and education are not producing a generation of people who are content. Japanese young people were found to have the lowest level of happiness of all 20 countries polled. Their most important value was listed as "working hard to help myself get on in life," but why do these values seem to be unfulfilling? It is because the emphasis on hard work and discipline is neglecting a crucial element of life, that is, fulfilling the longings of the heart. This report demonstrates the need for young people to have more than just instructions on how to live. What they need is parents and teachers who provide attention, positive input, and emotional support.

One key finding is that students whose parents reported spending time talking to their child daily or eating a main meal with their child at the table were 22–39% more likely to report high life satisfaction levels. Victimization of bullying is also less frequently reported by students who said they receive parental support when facing school difficulties. Students in schools with above-average well-being levels report much more support from teachers than those in schools with below-average well-being.[3]

The situation the youth of Japan find themselves in today demonstrates the truth of what the Bible teaches, namely, when the longings of the heart are not fulfilled, people are unstable. Information and education thrown at them will not make their well-being better. When parents stop to listen and engage their children, and when teachers spend time encouraging the students by showing personal interest, up to 40% of the students indicate high levels of life satisfaction. Those who did not get much attention only scored 17% satisfaction according to the results of the report.[4]

God created people with heartfelt needs. The attention given by adults and parents did encourage the students. Even so, adult and parental attention is not adequate to fill young people's deepest needs. It is not until we let God into our hearts that we discover what we are seeking. When God is filling our deepest longings, we find what we are really desiring.

When we experience the fullness of God, a new journey begins. It is a journey where our hearts grow in love with God and learn to praise and worship Him daily. The more time we spend reflecting on the beauty, grace, and greatness of God, the more our hearts will desire to place Him at the center of our lives. The things of this world, both good and bad, will have less attraction and less power to pull us away from Him.

The danger of taking our focus off our heart affections is what encouraged me to write this book. My view of Mt. Fuji was blocked that morning when I was enjoying the view. The car ride seemed beautiful and exciting until my view was blocked. I determined that moment that I need to take great care not to allow anything to block my view of God. I realized that the consequences of not looking to this gracious God would make my heart grow cold towards Him. I would be tempted to fill my heart with other things. This experience of looking at Mt. Fuji was only a single day in my life, but by spending time each day in praise and worship, God's love and grace seemed more real to me. Through reading the Word of God, meditation, and worship for the specific purpose of engaging my heart and not just to fulfill my daily duty, His presence was closer. I became convinced that when I take time to do this, the Holy Spirit applies His Word to my heart and I can offer praise and worship back to Him.

He will use the convicting words of God to show us idols and encourage us to confess them. The experience of the Father's kind, patient, accepting heart is what convinces us to let go of idols and put Him first in our lives. And the Spirit will convince us that God is sufficient to meet all our needs.

God has called us to be worshipers of Him, and He gives us an important tool to help. The Scriptures guide our minds and direct our thoughts in many ways every time we read them. Through the Bible, we never run out of words to speak to God, and our prayers will not be boring but full of variety and depth. And importantly, they will be God-centered prayers rather than focused on self. When prayer becomes primarily a time to tell God how great He is and thank Him, then our personal time of worship becomes vibrant and not boring. It transforms our hearts and lives. It is not just a duty but a privilege to meet with our Lord daily, whether just for a few minutes or an hour. It is a time that warms our hearts and encourages us to love Him faithfully.

CHANGE OUR SELF-IMAGE

In the previous chapter, we discussed how the view of ourselves changes when we accept our new status in Christ as freely given. This is so important that it is worth repeating. There is nothing in the world that can provide this new healthy self-image other than the gospel. The world teaches that we develop a good and healthy self-image through success—making good grades, succeeding in school, being popular with friends, getting into a good college, holding a good job, having successful children, etc. These are some ways we obtain a positive self-image. There is a problem with this value system, however. Sometimes when successful people achieve self-confidence, they become harsh, judgmental, and impatient with those who do not. And what will happen to those who cannot become successful in their own eyes? How can these people build a healthy self-image? They cannot measure up to their own standard of success, so they live with a sense of inadequacy and jealousy of those who succeed. High suicide rates, bullying at school and in the office, and drop out rates are evidence that there needs to be a better way for both the successful and unsuccessful to gain a healthy self-image.

The gospel provides the perfect answer. It is a standard for building one's self-image that anyone can reach. In the gospel, we are all failures before God because we do not keep His standards. In fact, we are worse than we think. When we look at our motivations, even our best efforts to be good are tainted with selfishness, pride, and lack of love for God and others. The apostle Paul, who we think of as being a great Christian, said about himself that he was the chief of sinners. But this did not destroy his self-image. In fact, it directed him to the answer we all need to cling to. Even though we are sinners and failures, God looks down on us and tells us that we are successful because of Jesus's righteousness. We are loved more than we dare dream possible. While unsuccessful in our attempts to be obedient, Jesus was successful for us. This is our new identity, and we all qualify to have it.

The truly amazing thing about this new self-image is that it makes us confident and humble at the same time. We can be confident because our new self-image is given through what Christ has done and not through what we have accomplished. We are humble and patient with others, loving them in their failures because we know that we are no different. The confidence the world gives produces pride and a judgmental attitude. The gospel, however, will grow in us humble and compassionate hearts toward others.

BECOME THE NEW CREATION

When we turn to Christ for forgiveness through faith, there is a radical change that takes place in our hearts. It is both an immediate and life-long process because we have become a new creation.

"Therefore, if anyone is in Christ, he is a new creation. The old has passed away; behold, the new has come." (II Corinthians 5:17)

What does this "new creation" look like? Here are some of the differences between our old self before Christ and the new creation when we are in Christ.

Changed Self

(Old = Old self before Christ)
(New = New creation in Christ)

Old — Outsider and under shame
New — Close to God and right with Him

Old — Under self-condemnation
New — Forgiven and accepted

Old — Under guilt and disapproval
New — Justified and living under the smile of approval

Old — Alone
New — Adopted by God into His family

Old — Incapable of change and dead
New — Capable of change and alive

Old — Bondage to discouragement
New — Saved by God freely by grace

Old — Diligent effort results in pride or envy
New — Accepted by grace and given the Spirit to change

Old — Salvation is earned
New — Salvation is received

Old — Daily life is not fulfilling
New — Future hope gives meaning to today and tomorrow

Changed World View

Old — My primary group is my family
New — My identity is my new family in Christ, my church

Old — Look to the world for praise
New — Look to Christ for praise

Old — My life is the center of my world
New — My life, money, time, and family belongs to God

Old — My beliefs and behavior are private
New — My faith is public, glorifying God in all of life

Changed Heart

Old — Closed, hardened heart to God
New — Open, warm heart ready to listen

Old — God is a scary policeman to obey
New — God is a kind, loving heavenly Father to live for

Old — Self-sufficient and full of pride
New — Trusting and dependent on God's grace

Old — Calls on God in times of need and wants
New — Calls on God for praise and worship

Old — Dutifully obeys to bring blessing
New — Joyfully obeys and seeks the God of blessing

Old — Covers or denies faults
New — Fearlessly confesses sins God and others

Changed Motivations

Old — Does good to look good before others
New — Does good to love God and is secure in His love

Old — Does good to feel good about oneself
New — Does good because God has forgiven

Old — Does good to bargain with God
New — Does good because God has already blessed

Changed Perspective

Old — Beauty in the world relaxes
New — Beauty in the world points to God

Old — Art and hobbies are for self-expression
New — Art and hobbies show God's creative nature

Old — Art is used to confirm one's self-worth
New — Art is something to be enjoyed under God's smiling
     face

Old — Life is short so live for now
New — Life is short but there is an eternity with God

Old — The world is cruel and unfair
New — In God's new world there are no tears or wrongs

These differences cannot begin to adequately summarize the changes that take place in our lives when we become children of God. The changes are to be enjoyed with God, but they are also to be enjoyed as a family. We do not view the mountain of the God of grace in private. We have brothers and sisters and spiritual mothers and fathers. Our experience with God grows deeper within the family as we worship and share and talk. The changes God desires to take place in our hearts are more dynamic and permanent when we do life together. We remain healthier and stronger within the family. This is what we need in order to keep our eyes on the gospel of God's grace. We know God's love in a deeper way when we share His love with others. What is God's plan? For believers to grow as active members of Christ's family, the local church.

CHAPTER 4

HOW CAN WE BE CONTINUALLY MOTIVATED TO LOOK AT THIS GOD OF GRACE?

Those who live in the towns of Fuji and Shimizu live in the shadow of Mt. Fuji. Yet, it is usually in the background. There are days and weeks when they do not even stop to look at or are even aware that the mountain is there.

We, too, while living in the presence of the God who created all things and whose beauty is beyond words can become like the citizens of Fuji and Shimizu. God is there, but for various reasons we stop looking. Whether or not we look at Mt. Fuji does not make any difference in our lives. But as we have already noted, it does make an enormous difference when we look to God. He is not just beautiful but is the One who has forgiven us and brought us into His family with blessings and promises for this life and all eternity. Thus, we praise and worship Him and owe Him our very lives. We may think that in light of all these blessings in Christ Jesus we would never let our eyes be taken off Him or let our hearts worship something or someone else...but we do! We need to be reminded to keep our eyes fixed on Jesus.

"Since we are surrounded by so great a cloud of witnesses,
let us also lay aside every weight, and sin which clings so

closely, and let us run with endurance the race that is set before us, looking to Jesus, the founder and perfecter of our faith, who for the joy that was set before him endured the cross, despising the shame, and is seated at the right hand of the throne of God." (Hebrews 12:1–2)

Paul challenges us in the same way.

"For this reason I bow my knees before the Father, from whom every family in heaven and on earth is named, that according to the riches of his glory he may grant you to be strengthened with power through his Spirit in your inner being, so that Christ may dwell in your hearts through faith —that you, being rooted and grounded in love, may have strength to comprehend with all the saints what is the breadth and length and height and depth, and to know the love of Christ that surpasses knowledge, that you may be filled with all the fullness of God." (Ephesians 3:14–19)

Notice the progression. First, we look to Christ as "a cloud of witnesses." We are members of God's family. We are part of "every family," all the saints and to all generations. Next, it is not enough to know about Jesus but are to love Him in "our inner being with our hearts." When we love Christ personally, we "know the love of Christ" and are "filled with the fullness of God." Lastly, we look to Jesus in hope of the future where we see Christ seated at "the right hand of God." In summary, Paul instructs us to look to Jesus as family, with love for Him in our hearts and with a hope in the future.

LOOK TO JESUS AS MEMBERS OF HIS FAMILY

Anyone brought up in Japanese society has received good training on how to be a loyal member of a group, whether to one's classmates, company, or family. They learned that one's importance is found in contributing to the well-being of the whole group. Loyalty is expected even at the cost of personal sacrifice or loss of freedom.

The Bible makes it clear that loyalty to a group is important. We run this race of life not primarily as individuals but as part of God's family. Following Christ means finding identity in the family of God. Though we believe Christ's death on the cross is for individual salvation, this does not mean that faith is just a private matter. Christ is Lord of all nations, and we all belong to a new family. We do not act just as individuals but must reflect on the character of this new family and the effect our actions have on it.

An individual's desire for praise and approval is what usually motivates people to avoid shame and gain approval. But in this new family, shame and honor take on new meaning. Shame is no longer used as a weapon to control behavior. The shame of our failures has been taken by Jesus. It no longer has power over us when we see the shame Jesus faced on the cross. Deliverance from shame and guilt has become the common shared experience and identity. It is the foundation for our shared experience. God's forgiveness and acceptance is what removes the fear of shame and ties the family together.

When we become members of the family of Christ, we have been given a common identity that unites us. Our identity as forgiven children of God makes us thankful, and our desire is to give God praise and obedience. When temptations face us and it becomes difficult to obey God, it makes a big difference that we are members of a family, where we are cared for through encouragement, advice, and prayer.

We can see the God of grace more clearly as a member of Christ's body. This is why God has instructed us to express our faith in public and not just in private. Our faith is not just a private matter between ourselves as individual Christians and God. To show the private nature of faith, He made our baptism ceremony to be a public expression of our faith. Baptism is a public announcement that in committing our life to Christ, we have become a new family member in the family of God in our local church. It is not a private act but a public one.

Partaking in communion too is a public act. We are together acknowledging our mutual need to place our faith both in the body of Christ broken for us and in His blood shed on the cross. Communion is not to be observed as an individual act where one is focused only on private sins. The cup we drink is drunk together as a family who is thankful for the gift of Christ's atonement. It is observed where we are aware of the family around us with whom we share oneness. Communion is a "holy meal" (聖餐式) and should not be taken lightly. It is a time to reflect on our sins, confess them to Christ, and rejoice in our forgiveness. But it is also celebrated as a "family meal" (家族餐式) and is a profound way we experience our togetherness as a family. Together, we confess our need of the cross. Together, we rejoice in God's forgiveness and live in the smile of His love. Together, we experience what Noah did when God put his family on the ark and saved them all.

So, too, every time we observe communion with our family of spiritual brothers and sisters, we experience over and over again God's grace which has placed us as a family in His boat of salvation. God used a large boat to save Noah's family and today He uses the body of Christ in order to help us grow in sanctification. We are to glorify God and live in His presence as members of one big family encouraging each other to good works.

SEE CHURCH AS A HOSPITAL FOR THE SICK AND NEEDY

It sounds good to say that every Christian is a part of the body of Christ, a member of this family. There are those, however, who call themselves Christians but do not join or even attend a church. When asked why, some say that they had a bad experience and don't want to go back. Their thinking is that since it is a place where the love of God is taught, then it should be a perfect place. But rather, the church is more like a hospital where the sick come to get healed.

God has called together into His family all sorts of people with varying degrees of problems and backgrounds. Many bring with them their needs and problems that will challenge the church. But Jesus said in Mark 2:17 that he has come not for the healthy but for the sick: "It is not the healthy who need a doctor, but the sick. I have not come to call the righteous, but sinners" (NIV). This is why the local church resembles a hospital. It is often a place where those who are not emotionally healthy come, because it is a safe place and they know that they will be accepted. This makes for the potential of messy relationships and hurt feelings.

The only way for a church to be a safe place for the sick to attend is for each member to extend to others the patience and gracious love they received from God. They must see how the gospel applies to them. This means always remembering how they too are sinners who are loved because of Jesus Christ and not worthy of God's forgiveness and love. When we see that everyone in the church is there because of the grace of God, then there is no reason to judge or reject others. Only when the "cross" (十) is central to what we "think" or "believe" (思), can we understand the true meaning of "grace" (恵).

The Japanese *kanji* for grace shows that the cross is central to the identity of every Christian (十 + 思 = 恵). When we understand this, we can say along with Paul, "But far be it from me to boast except in the cross of our Lord Jesus Christ, by which the world has been crucified to me, and I to the world" (Galatians 6:14). Since we are all sick people forgiven through Christ's death on the cross, we have no reason to be judgmental, unforgiving, or impatient with those who attend church or who are difficult to get along with.

The ability to have healthy, loving, and patient relationships within the church depends upon each member believing that the gospel applies to them. They must never forget they are sinners who are loved more than they realize because of Jesus Christ and not because they have proved themselves worthy of God's forgiveness.

When we see that there is a cross in the center of the character for grace (恵), this helps us to remember we all deserve judgment and rejection from God. It can help us to be humble and more forgiving and patient with those difficult people who attend our church.

Japanese society does not accept this fundamental teaching of Christianity. Religion is understood to be only for the weak who cannot make it on their own and need organized religion to get through life. Although they might face difficulties, they think they are living a good life and can manage on their own. And thus, they are not sick and do not need a "hospital." This thinking towards religion is strongly imbedded in the minds of many who live in Japan. Consequently, even after becoming a Christian and joining a church, there tends to be resistance to admitting our weaknesses and need for help. It is hard to talk about struggles and ask others for help. This is true even though they know with their minds that it is God's purpose to call us out of the world of sorrow, pain, sickness, loneliness, and disappointments to bring us into the church where we can be safe from the harsh, disapproving looks and be shown compassion.

Apart from the church facing challenges from difficult members, it faces other challenges because of multiple generations, children, teenagers, college students, mothers, company workers, and the elderly. Each generation has its own perspective on life, yet all are called to worship and fellowship together harmoniously. There are also people of different education levels, social levels, and wealth bringing additional challenges. Normally, people seek out friendships with those alike in age, status, and interests, but Christ calls all sorts of people together to be one in Him.

While difficult, it provides interaction with fellow Christians who are different from us in many ways. It is a blessing to know someone who we would otherwise never meet. I remember cleaning our church Saturday morning with other members of the church. Next to me was the vice-president of the Honda car factory. In Christ, we are all equal and can enjoy each other's company and learn and be encouraged.

We all bring life experiences and differing perspectives and can enjoy sharing them with each other. As we get older, it is good to be with young people to be reminded of what it was like when we first became believers. This helps us to be less critical and more patient and understanding. And it is good for young students to talk to adults who care about them and offer encouragement and a listening ear.

We have considered two challenges to the church, the stigma that religion is only for the weak and the challenge of diversity. The third challenge is the church's desire to have and maintain *ittaikan*, a strong peaceful unity. Church members want their church to be a safe, comfortable place, and outsiders can be a threat to this oneness. This has caused some churches to turn inward and look at outsiders with caution. They may not consciously want to exclude others from coming to their church, but fear has made some newcomers feel unwelcome.

My conversation with a young college teacher serves as an example. After my sermon, she asked me to provide someone to come to her campus to do evangelism. She did not feel free to ask her students to come to her church to hear the gospel because of the way her students looked. They were art students and many had body-piercings, dyed hair, and punk rock hair styles. They looked rebellious to the average person but were genuinely serious about life and asked deep questions which she felt inadequate to answer. Even though they were eager to listen to answers to their questions, if brought to her church she feared her students would not be understood or accepted. The sad part of this story is that if these students had looked more like a Waseda University student with normal clothes and hair style, they would have been welcomed.

Churches have a great opportunity to welcome outsiders. It is said that more Japanese living abroad than those in Japan become interested in Christianity, study the Bible, and attend church. This is a wonderful way God is reaching Japanese with the gospel, but there is a problem when they return to their own country. When they start attending a local church as Japanese who have been "Westernized," they are suspect and do not always feel welcomed. This reluctance to open doors to this group of people has given birth to a new term *"kikokusha*-friendly churches," or "returnee-friendly" churches. There is a network of churches formed throughout Japan that welcome returnees and assist them in readjustment.

How does a church learn to be welcoming? It begins when the church sees itself as a hospital where all sorts of people are welcomed, safe, loved, and accepted. A hospital does not have the right to turn away sick patients and neither does the church. By opening doors to all who want to come in, the church is testifying to the power of God's grace.

UNDERSTAND DANGERS OF INDIVIDUALISM

In addition to the church in Japan facing the challenge of keeping doors open to outsiders, it faces another challenge with the modern movement of young people towards *jikojitsugen* (individualism). Previous generations held to traditional values of loyalty to one's group where pressure from the outside determines one's actions. But there is a shift away from these values with the younger generation. While this modern trend towards making decisions as an individual has made it easier for a young person to go against the wishes of parents and become a Christian, there are down sides. The focus has changed to self-fulfillment. Whereas traditional values restrict the pursuit of one's own life, personal fulfillment is more important than conforming to the demands of the group. In light of this movement, it is understandable why it takes courage to believe that God is calling them to join a church. Their generation is telling them they will find personal fulfillment by living out their own dreams and putting oneself first. They are told that accountability and responsibility to live out lives together within a group hinders personal fulfillment.

It is important that the church today understand this shift in values among its young people. It must be willing to welcome diversity in its congregation while teaching God's plan for each to grow as a part of a local church. The welcoming group will encourage the young to join the church and to grow in their faith. Unfortunately, some churches have discouraged the young by insisting on carrying out old traditions even though the traditions are not taught in the Bible, such as one's physical appearance and allowing for only one style of church music. Other churches have focused on the youth in a compromising way. Their goal is to have the young attend services by making them popular, energetic, and entertaining. They seek to provide an emotional boost on Sundays with dynamic worship music and pep talk presentations to gear up their spirits to sustain them through the week. In making the focus of the service on meeting one's emotional needs, the unintentional result is the promotion of individualism and self-fulfillment rather than growth through strong commitment to the body of believers. In doing so, the emphasis is an appeal to emotionalism and individual happiness more than loyalty to Christ through a local church.

BE PART OF THE CHURCH

We discussed the dangers of the modern movement towards individualism, but we are not saying there is no individual aspect to the gospel. Christ died for each person's sin. Everyone is personally responsible to repent and is forgiven through faith in Jesus. And we are all individually made new in Christ to live for Him. Only Christ can give us the individual experience of freedom from condemnation and loneliness. Our faith is a private matter between God and us. We must trust in God and no one can do that for us.

This emphasis on the importance of each person's responsibility to respond to the gospel individually does not give the believer a reason to refrain from joining a church for accountability. We are to grow in our walk with Christ through Christian fellowship. The church is where our faith and walk with Jesus becomes more real to us as we share our thoughts and experiences with other believers who understand and care.

When we share our experiences with others, they have greater impact in our lives. This has been my experience in the story about my view of Mt. Fuji being blocked. The emotions, my thoughts which I experienced over 15 years ago, still seem very real today since I have shared them with many people. If I had kept it to myself, it would not have had this ongoing impact in my life and I would have forgotten about it long ago. My story illustrates why it is important to be a part of the body of Christ. As we share experiences of our walk with Jesus, it becomes more real to us. We learn from them and so do others. When retelling our story with others our hearts are encouraged and strengthened.

Over the years, I have talked to people who have stopped going to church for various reasons. Some tell me, "I can read and pray by myself." Others say, "I'm too busy to go to church." But perhaps the saddest is this, "It's easier to be a *kakure* 'hidden' Christian, because when I'm alone there are no expectations placed on me by others." As I continue my conversation with these individuals, I soon find that their faith has not grown over the years. Their relationship with God has become impersonal. Few still read their Bible, and their prayer life consists of calling to God only when they are in deep need.

There is nothing more dangerous to spiritual health than to stop attending church. It is true we can read the Bible, pray, and worship God away from church, but because our hearts are "deceitful above all things, and desperately sick; who can understand it?" (Jeremiah 17:9), we cannot rely only on ourselves to let the Bible speak into our lives. We need the input of others. Left to our own thinking, we will make a god unto ourselves, a god after our liking but not the God of the Bible. This self-created god will not challenge our beliefs or how we are living. We need people who are faithful to the Bible to speak truth to us. They challenge us to live in a godly manner and when facing trials, they can reassure us with their caring hearts and prayers. (Appendix #1 is a sample guide to devotional time using Scripture to guide thoughts and prayers.)

WALK WITH CHRIST BOTH AT HOME AND IN THE CHURCH

There are two sides to the Christian life. One is loyalty to church and the other is our private walk with God at home. Both are important but it is often the latter which is ignored. We are called by God to be part of the body of Christ, but this does not exclude the need for each Christian to spend time alone with God in a consistent and disciplined way. Jesus modeled this for us by regularly going away by himself to a quiet place. If our lives are to be shaped and molded and our hearts are to be protected from growing cold and hard, there is no substitute for spending time alone reading the Bible, meditating on it, and letting it guide our praise and prayer. The purpose of this time is to remember His grace on a regular basis. Hearts made thankful for Christ will grow in the desire to love and obey Him. The goal each day is to remember God's love and have our hearts touched by Him.

SHAPE YOUR HEART AFFECTIONS

Japan is one of the most highly educated countries in the world, but something more than education is needed—a heart transformed by the gospel message. This is the only thing that can change someone from the inside. Our lives change when our hearts find purpose in God. One writer put it this way,

> "Our heart is the seat of our longings and desires. You are
> what you love because you live toward what you want. . . .
> We all have our idea of what a good life is and this is shaped
> by our daily practices. How we spend our time, our money,
> our friends, our hobbies, etc. all these draw our heart affections and determine how we live."[1]

The focus on the heart is not just a Western idea. The heart is clearly central to emotion and action as seen in various Japanese *kanji*. The radical 心 (heart) is used in many words: fear (恐れ), anger (怒り), love (愛), sadness (悲しさ), shame (恥じ), worry (心配), and others. From ancient times, people understood how heart affections strongly influence feelings and actions. Yet, the teaching in school and society's attempts to control human behavior ignore the heart by appealing to rules, guidelines, and instructions. The assumption is that if you explain how to live a good life, this information will shape actions.

Since our hearts are shaped by habits, we need to regularly spend time alone with God. We are controlled by what we love. The more our hearts are moved to love God the less they are pulled away from Him to look elsewhere for fulfillment. When our hearts are shaped and molded through praise and worship, our reactions to things and our attitudes toward people change. The Spirit within us takes these truths that we focus on through the habit of meditating on Him through the Word. This will change us to have a more Christ-like loving heart. We learn to love, then, not primarily by acquiring information but rather through practices that form the habits that grow our love for God and others.

The benefits of how God shapes our hearts through practicing daily spiritual discipline cannot be over emphasized. A powerful illustration can be found in the famous story of the US Airlines pilot, Captain Sully. On January 15, 2009, Sully took off from LaGuardia Airport, and when he reached the altitude of 2,800 feet, his plane flew into a flock of geese. Both engines stalled and he had only three minutes to land the plane without crashing and killing all the passengers and crew. He was able to make hundreds of decisions perfectly in order to glide his plane onto the Hudson River without breaking apart and killing everyone. People were amazed that he could make these decisions within three minutes in order to redirect his powerless airplane onto the Hudson River. No one was even injured! People called it a miracle, but for Captain Sully it was the fruit of many thousands of hours in the air and hours of practice as a gliding instructor that prepared him for that moment. When the emergency confronted him, the habits that shaped his ability to respond quickly took over and all were saved.

Captain Sully's years of training and experience show how important it is to shape our hearts through practice. It may seem strange to talk of our time with God in reading, studying His Word, prayer, and worship as "practice," but this is what it is. Practice is what shapes habits in our lives enabling us to face unexpected moments in a way that is pleasing to God. Through the time we spend in praise and worship, we can learn patience with difficult people, face hardships with faith, resist temptations, and live unselfishly for God and others.

Some may disagree with this emphasis on discipline, saying that it relies on man's works rather than faith. "Simply pray to God to change you, and he'll do it. It's a matter of faith!" We have heard the testimony of brothers and sisters who were instantly changed when they gave their lives to Christ. God may choose to change people overnight in a supernatural way, but this does not negate the principle that our lives are shaped by what we love.

It pleases the Lord when we seek Him with our hearts through regular, disciplined time. This grows our love for God and enables us to experience the power of the Spirit over time. Which brings greater pleasure and glory to God? A quick change through a miracle or being changed through time with Christ in close fellowship? God desires a loving relationship where we daily walk in dependence and loving fellowship with Him.

LOOK TO THE MOUNTAIN

The following four habits are practical suggestions of how we can strengthen our faith for the purpose of engaging our hearts—the seat of affections that shape our actions and worship.

1. Spend time reading the Bible and in worshipful prayer reminding yourself of God's glory in Jesus Christ. Let your heart be moved by His amazing love. (See Appendix 1 for the prayer guide.)
2. Spend less time on media and more time focusing your mind on Christ. There are books, devotionals, sermons, and music to listen to throughout the day. Don't let society mold you into its form or let your mind and heart be consumed by all that it encounters. We should be concerned about world events, its values, history, and society, but they should not control us.
3. Attend church for worship and fellowship to encourage yourself and others to look at Christ and get involved. Pray for your heart to be engaged.
4. Find a small group of people you can talk with and pray with. Ask God to give you a brother or sister in Christ with whom you can share your thoughts and struggles, and who can encourage you to stay faithful to God.

CONCLUSION

WE HAVE INVESTIGATED FOUR ELEMENTS of looking to the great mountain of the God of grace. In Chapter 1, we looked at who God is. In Chapter 2, we considered how this God graciously provides for all our emotional needs. In Chapter 3, we saw what happens when we look to this God and how we are changed. And in Chapter 4, we talked about why the motivation for looking at God is so important, because God is interested in changing our hearts and not just external actions.

Japanese society is profoundly moralistic. Even for Christians, it is easy to be influenced by this social standard where one is evaluated by actions good or bad. It is learned from early childhood and continues throughout life. The fear of isolation and rejection and shame of failure and the duty to be loyal to one's group have been used to motivate daily behavior.

The important challenge for Christians living in this moralistic society of Japan is to clearly understand how we are changed. In this book, we asserted that while fear, shame, and moral duty can bring about some degree of change, it does so only by constraining external behavior. External pressures cannot change the heart, and real change comes from inside a changed heart. This is why we ask for the motivation behind one's behavior. A person can be polite while hating on the inside, but the gospel of Christ can change the heart.

It is my prayer that we will all learn to look at our God of grace to daily grow in appreciation for what He has done, rest in His accomplishment, and grow in our love for Him and others.

Q: How are you righteous before God?

A: Only by true faith in Jesus Christ. Even though my conscience accuses me of having grievously sinned against all God's commandments, of never having kept any of them, and of still being inclined toward all evil, nevertheless, without any merit of my own, out of sheer grace, God grants and credits to me the perfect satisfaction, righteousness, and holiness of Christ, as if I had never sinned nor been a sinner, and as if I had been as perfectly obedient as Christ was obedient for me. All I need to do is accept this gift with a believing heart. (Heidelberg Catechism Question #60)

We are changed through faith in what Christ has done for us. We need to let this truth sink down into our minds and hearts daily. When our identity is founded on who we are in Christ, we are protected from discouragement, self-condemnation, loneliness, pride, self-dependency, and all other destructive forces that come from within us and outside us.

In light of what God has done for us in Christ Jesus, we are enabled to run our race with joy and confidence. And Jesus is the mountain of grace that we look to daily.

"Let us run with endurance the race that is set before us,

looking to Jesus, the founder and perfecter of our faith, who for the joy that was set before him endured the cross, despising the shame, and is seated at the right hand of the throne of God." (Hebrews 12:1–2)

ACKNOWLEDGMENTS

I would like to express my gratitude for the people who have helped shape my thinking and gave me the vision and desire to write this book. From childhood, I had a father who taught me to think about ways Christianity offered answers to Japanese society. My teenage years were influenced by the HiBA (High School Born-Againers) Christian youth program where I had an opportunity to live out my faith in community and see gospel change in the lives of my Japanese friends. Pastor Horikoshi taught me how to speak and teach in simple, practical terms the importance of setting our faith on the understanding of a Creator Lord.

I am thankful for the men and women in the Presbyterian Church of Japan with whom I have had the privilege of working. They have been kind and patient in their dealings with me. Steve Childers helped me understand spiritual formation and church planting. Tim Keller continues to instruct in a clear way how the gospel changes and empowers the human heart to serve out of grateful obedience. The Lord has allowed me to learn from all these men and women, leaving an influence reflected throughout this book.

Finally, my wife, Susan, who walked with me through each of these steps over the past 45 years, has encouraged me in many ways to write the thoughts and experiences in this book. And together we say, the most helpful training we received to under-stand the implications of the gospel of grace as it applies to every area of our lives has been through Sonship training. There we experienced simple truths of the gospel move from our heads to our hearts in a profoundly deep and personal way.

All these have been gifts from the Lord for which we are most grateful. Thanks and praise belong to our gracious God and Father!

APPENDIX #1 CONTEMPLATIVE PRAYER

ALLOW YOUR INNER SELF TO BE quiet and still. Look to God in a state of utter reverence, admiration, and whole-hearted worship. Focus on Him and be moved in response to His wonderful grace and beauty.[1]

PREPARATION

Stop to realize God's presence. Focus your attention on Him and seek illumination.

READ THE WORD

- Read the text slowly 3–4 times. What is the context? What is the outline?
- Place yourself in the narrative accounts. In the discourse passages, ask the significance of the repetition and comparisons. Who is causing what?
- What does the passage teach about God, Christ, yourself, and what you should be or do? Are there examples, commands, promises?

- List the teachings that strike you.

MEDITATIVE PRAYER

Listen to the Lord God and let the text ask you questions in four categories which can be remembered by the acrostic ACTS: A — Adore, C — Confess, T — Thank, S — Seek.

- A — How can I *adore* and love God on the basis of this? What can I praise Him for?
- C — What can I *confess* to God on the basis of this? What are my wrong behaviors, harmful emotions, or false attitudes?
- T — How can I *thank* Christ as the ultimate revelation of this attribute of God and answer to this sin or need?
- S — How can *seek* God to change me as this truth becomes powerfully real to me?

AFFECTIVE PRAYER

Remove the affections of your heart off false objects and offer your heart to the Lord.

- Return to the prayers of confession above. How do these sins come from an inordinate hope for someone or something to give you satisfaction that only Jesus can give? Repent for grieving Him and ignoring Him.
- Thank Christ for giving you so much more fully and appropriately than the very things you are looking for elsewhere. Rejoice and think of what He has done and what He has given you.
- Offer up your heart and surrender your will.
- Create a watchword to remember all day.

CONTEMPLATIVE PRAYER

Sense the absolute adequacy and excellence of the Lord.

- Continue to rejoice in the aspect of Christ's sufficiency and excellence that has become most real, vivid, and relevant to you. Admire Him and wonder at His Greatness. This is not a chatting and analysis time. If you find yourself moved to inner song, sing His praises!
- Ask yourself: (1) What does this passage show of His majesty and greatness? (2) What does this show of His grace, loveliness, and sweetness? (3) What does this show of His wisdom and depth?
- Praise and adore Him along these lines, "How did I neglect or miss such wonder, love, grace, and greatness in You?"
- Begin your prayers of petition.

APPENDIX #2 NEW SELF-IMAGE THROUGH GOSPEL CHANGE

CONFIDENCE (when successful)[1]

- Have to be competitive to maintain self-worth
- Self-absorption leads to self-confidence and condescension

HUMILIATION (when unsuccessful)

- Prone to give up after failure and envious of successful people
- Self-absorption can lead to self-disdain and shyness

GOSPEL UNDERSTANDING

- Boasting in the cross (Galatians 6:14)
- Knowing oneself to be a bigger sinner than imagined
- Knowing oneself to be more loved and accepted in Christ than ever dreamed possible

WHEN WE BELIEVE THE GOSPEL

- Enormously bold
- Accepted and loved in Christ
- Not demoralized by rejection and criticism (because the only one who ultimately counts accepts me)
- No inferiority complex or envy (because it is sufficient that my Father accepts me)
- Does not serve out of personal needs (because ministry to others flows from Christ's love)
- Freed to confront in love and take risks (because secure in Christ and do not need to protect my own record when attacked)
- Hope for everyone because it's God's grace that saves and changes people

WHEN WE FORGET THE GOSPEL

- Fearful and insecure
- Look to own performance rather than Christ's performance
- Fearful of rejection and criticism, demobilizes (because it's scary to risk losing respect)
- Feel inferior to and envious of success of others (because I seem to be the one always messing up)
- Try to help fill personal need (and feel overly fulfilled and important when helping others)
- Too threatened to risk rejection by confronting others
- Very selective about who to reach out to because some people are beyond hope of ever being reached, and thinking what's the use even trying, because they'll never change

UTTERLY SENSITIVE AND BOLD

- I know I am a big sinner

- Can sympathize, identify, and reach out (because outside of Christ I am no different)
- Do not look down in judgment of others (because I am saved only by grace and not by my own goodness)
- Am not co-dependent and do not run from hard relationships when unfulfilling (because I am fulfilled in Christ and want to give)
- Courteous and not pushy or coercing (because I am looking to God to change people)

INSENSITIVE AND PROUD

- Lose sight of own sinfulness
- Lose touch with the pain of sins and need to be humble (because have overcome and don't do that anymore)
- Cannot avoid being impatient and judgmental with the "weak" (wondering why they can't change and stop doing the same thing)
- Co-dependent and give up quickly when there is little personal reward in the relationship (because need to get something back to pursue it)
- Impolite, pushy, and manipulative in relationships (because if don't use whatever means and time given right now, they may never believe or change)

ENDNOTES

PREFACE

1. Don Richardson, *The Peace Child*, 4th ed. (Ventura, CA: Regal Books, 2005) 256.

FOREWORD

1. Tim Keller, *the movement*, eNewsletter of the Redeemer Church Planting Center, August 2004.

2. WHAT BLOCKS OUR VIEW OF GOD?

1. Steven L. Childers explains eight predicaments of man that hinder his relationship with God and how applying gospel truths can remove and restore that close relationship. I am indebted to this teaching because it helped me see how these eight predicaments become "trees" that block our relationship in the Japanese context. Childers outlines these predicaments in *Global Church Advancement Manual*, New Church Network Meeting #5: Gospel Renewal & Prayer, (Orlando, FL: Global Church Advancement, Inc., 2003) 20.
2. Janet & Geoff Benge, *Count Zinzendorf: Firstfruit, Christian Heroes Then and Now*. (Seattle: YWAM Publishing, 2012) ebook.

3. HOW ARE WE CHANGED WHEN WE LOOK AT GOD?

1. Tim Keller, "Following Jesus" sermon series Redeemer Presbyterian Church, New York City, "Our Birth: Cosmic," May 4, 2014.
2. Redeemer Presbyterian Church, "Gospel Ministry and Idols" (2001). These principles are also outlined in two books now translated into Japanese, *The Prodigal God* and *Counterfeit Gods*.
3. "Role of Parents in the Well-Being of Students," *The Japan Times*, January 3, 2019.
4. www.oecd.org/pisa/PISA2015-Students-Well-being-Country-note-Japan.pdf. Accessed December 10, 2021.

4. HOW CAN WE BE CONTINUALLY MOTIVATED TO LOOK AT THIS GOD OF GRACE?

1. James K. A. Smith, *You Are What You Love: The Spiritual Power of Habit*. (Grand Rapids: Brazos Press, 2016) ebook.

APPENDIX #1 CONTEMPLATIVE PRAYER

1. Based on Tim Keller, "Adoring Christ III" D.Min. course Session 19, Reformed Theological Seminary, Orlando, February 1–5, 1999. Adapted by the author.

APPENDIX #2 NEW SELF-IMAGE THROUGH GOSPEL CHANGE

1. Based on *Paul's Letter to the Galatians: Living in Line with the Truth of the Gospel* by Tim Keller, Redeemer Presbyterian Church, Chapter 12 "Gospel Relationships" 2002. Adapted by the author.

ABOUT THE AUTHOR

Bruce Young is the third generation of Youngs to minister in Japan. Bruce's life in Japan began as a one-year-old when his parents fled from the Communist occupation of China in 1948. After graduating from Christian Academy in Japan, he attended Covenant College and Covenant Seminary, where he met his wife, Susan.

For the first twenty years of ministry in Japan, Bruce and Susan planted churches in Yokkaichi and Nagoya. For the next ten years, they mentored in spiritual renewal in the greater Tokyo area. For their last sixteen years, they served in the Spiritual Life Department of Mission to the World, mentoring missionaries all over the world while maintaining relationships in Japan as consultants.

In 2020, they retired from Mission to the World and now live near Chattanooga, Tennessee. They have three children and ten grandchildren.

FEEDBACK

Thank you for reading *Living in Full View of the God of Grace*. Would you please take a moment to share your thoughts on this book by leaving a review on Amazon and Goodreads? This will help others get a sense of what they can expect from this book and spread the word of how it has impacted you.

To leave a review on Amazon:

- Go to this book on Bruce's author page
(amazon.com/author/bruceyoung)
- Hover over the Amazon ratings and click on "See all customer reviews"
- Click on "Write a customer review"

You can also leave comments on social media (#livinginfullview) and connect with the publisher directly by writing info@communityarts.jp.

We look forward to hearing from you!

www.ingramcontent.com/pod-product-compliance
Lightning Source LLC
Chambersburg PA
CBHW021650120626
46545CB00002B/794